W9-BWX-503

Our "Compacted" Compact Clinicals Team

Dear Valued Customer,

Welcome to Compact Clinicals. We are committed to bringing mental health professionals up-to-date, diagnostic and treatment information in a compact, timesaving, easy-to-read format. Our line of books provides current, thorough reviews of assessment and treatment strategies for mental disorders.

We've "compacted" complete information for diagnosing each disorder and comparing how different theoretical orientations approach treatment. Our books use nonacademic language, real-world examples, and well-defined terminology.

Enjoy this and other timesaving books from Compact Clinicals.

Sincerely,

Melanie A. Dean

Melanie Dean, Ph.D.
President

Compact Clinicals New Line of Books

Compact Clinicals currently offers these condensed reviews for professionals:

- **Attention Deficit Hyperactivity Disorder (in Adults and Children):** The Latest Assessment and Treatment Strategies

- **Borderline Personality Disorder:** The Latest Assessment and Treatment Strategies

- **Conduct Disorders:** The Latest Assessment and Treatment Strategies

- **Major Depressive Disorder:** The Latest Assessment and Treatment Strategies

- **Obsessive-Compulsive Disorder:** The Latest Assessment and Treatment Strategies

- **Post Traumatic and Acute Stress Disorder:** The Latest Assessment and Treatment Strategies

---

Call for Writers

Compact Clinicals is always interested in publishing new titles in order to keep our selection of books current and comprehensive. If you have a book proposal or an idea you would like to discuss, please call or write to:

Melanie Dean, Ph.D., President
Compact Clinicals
7205 NW Waukomis Dr., Suite A
Kansas City, MO 64151
(816) 587-0044

Obsessive Compulsive Disorder

The Latest Assessment and Treatment Strategies

by
**Gail Steketee, Ph.D., Teresa A. Pigott, M.D.
& Todd Schemmel, Ph.D. cand.**

Compact Clinicals...*condensed reviews for professionals*

Obsessive Compulsive Disorder
The Latest Assessment and Treatment Strategies

by
Gail Steketee, Ph.D., Teresa A. Pigott, M.D.,
& Todd Schemmel, Ph.D. cand.

Published by: Compact Clinicals
7205 NW Waukomis Dr., Suite A
Kansas City, MO 64151
816-587-0044

Compact Clinicals...*condensed reviews for professionals*

Copy Editing and Desktop Publishing by:
In Credible English
1800 South West Temple, Suite 501-72
Salt Lake City, UT 84115
Cover Design by:
Patrick G. Handley

Library of Congress Cataloging in Publication data:
Obsessive compulsive disorder : the latest assessment and treatment
strategies / [edited] by Gail Steketee, Teresa A. Pigott & Todd
Schemmel.
P.   cm.
Includes bibliographical references and index.
ISBN 1-887537-12-0 (pbk).
1. Obsessive-compulsive disorder. I. Steketee, Gail.
II. Pigott, Teresa A., 1958-   . III. Schemmel, Todd, 1973-   .
[DNLM: 1. Obsessive-Compulsive Disorder--diagnosis. 2. Obsessive
-Compulsive Disorder--therapy.   WM 176 01456 1999]
RC533.0273 1999
616.85'227--dc21
DNLM/DLC
for Library of Congress   99-19852
                                                              CIP

ISBN 1-887537-12-0

Read Me First

As a mental health professional, often the information you need can only be obtained after countless hours of reading or library research. If your schedule precludes this time commitment, Compact Clinicals is the answer.

Our books and tapes are practitioner oriented with easy-to-read treatment descriptions and examples. Compact Clinicals books are written in a nonacademic style. Our books are formatted to make the first reading as well as ongoing reference quick and easy. You will find:

- *Anecdotes*—Each chapter begins and ends with a fictionalized account that personalizes the disorder. These accounts include a **"Dear Diary"** entry at the beginning of each chapter that illustrates a typical client's viewpoint about their disorder. Each chapter ends with **"File Notes"** of a fictional therapist, Pat Owen. These **"File Notes"** address assessment, diagnosis, and treatment considerations for the "client" writing the **"Dear Diary"** entries.

- *Sidebars*—Narrow columns on the outside of each page highlight important information, preview upcoming sections or concepts, and define terms used in the text.

- *Definitions*—Terms are defined in the sidebars where they originally appear in the text and in an alphabetical glossary on pages 91 through 94.

- *References*—Numbered references appear in the text following information from that source. Full references appear in a bibliography on pages 95 through 102.

- *Case Examples*—Our examples illustrate typical client comments or conversational exchanges that help clarify different treatment approaches. Identifying information in the examples (e.g., the individual's real name, profession, age, and/or location) has been changed to protect the confidentiality of those clients discussed in case examples.

Contents

Diary of Amy P.

May 4

I went to a therapist today. I can't stop thinking about awful things that could happen to my husband and my kids. I'm spending more and more time undoing and redoing almost everything I do. I'm starting to avoid the next task for fear of getting stuck in this pattern all over again. It's starting to affect my relationships and the amount of work I can handle.

Somebody please help me!

You will be following a typical client's thoughts about their disorder through the "Dear Diary" notes at the beginning of each chapter. At the end of each chapter, a fictional therapist's "File Notes" will reflect the assessment and treatment of the client writing the "Dear Diary" notes.

Chapter One: General Information About Obsessive Compulsive Disorder

What is Obsessive Compulsive Disorder (OCD)?

OCD is an anxiety disorder that involves recurrent obsessions or compulsions severe enough to be time consuming or cause great difficulty in every day life.[1] Obsessions are intrusive thoughts, impulses, or images, such as repetitive thoughts of violence or contamination. Compulsions or rituals, are repetitive, intentional behaviors that one feels compelled to perform, often reluctantly. Compulsions are performed in response to an obsession and are intended to neutralize or prevent some feared event. Common compulsions include excessive washing, which neutralizes fears of contamination, and checking, which neutralizes fears of potential disasters occurring. Other rituals include repeating actions to prevent harm, ordering objects to achieve symmetry, and performing mental rituals.

Written for the professional, this book presents general information about OCD in chapter 1, diagnostic information in chapter 2, environmental treatments of OCD in chapter 3, and biological treatments in chapter 4.

How Common is OCD?

Obsessive Compulsive Disorder (OCD), previously considered a very rare mental disorder, now appears to be a hidden epidemic. Recent research indicates that over 6.5 million people suffer from OCD, making it one of the most common mental disorders.[1]

Recent studies indicate that OCD impacts about one adult in 40 or 2.5 percent of the general population at some point in their lives.[2] OCD symptoms usually begin during late adolescence or early adulthood, but may begin in childhood. Between one-third and two-thirds of people with OCD have associated significant life events or stresses at the onset of the disorder, such as the death of a family member, pregnancy, childbirth, or sexual problems.[3] Additional characteristics include indications that:

This chapter answers the following:

- **What is Obsessive Compulsive Disorder (OCD)?** — *This section defines OCD and some common associated compulsions and obsessions.*

- **How Common is OCD?** — *This section illustrates the number of people with the disorder and notes differences in OCD between men and women.*

- **What is the Likelihood of Recovery?** — *This section discusses the severity and outcome of the disorder with and without treatment.*

- Slightly more than half of those with OCD are women.[2]

- People with OCD have above average intelligence.[4]

- Peak age of onset for males is between 13 and 15 years old.[2]

- Peak age of onset for females is between 20 and 24 years old.[2]

- Onset usually occurs gradually.

Many OCD sufferers wait years before seeking treatment. On average, a person waits seven years after first experiencing significant symptoms to get help.[2] This hesitancy to seek treatment may result from shame and embarrassment because people with OCD are often unaware that many others experience similar symptoms.

Approximately 50 percent of married individuals with OCD report marital discord resulting from their disorder.[2]

Quality of life for OCD sufferers is generally much worse than for the general population.[5] Many sufferers experience significant functional impairment, such as an inability to work or maintain relationships because they spend most of the day performing rituals. This behavior often results in job loss, marital disruption, and loss of other interpersonal relationships. In fact, the earlier onset of OCD in men may be responsible for their unusually low marriage rate (only 25 percent).[6]

What is the Likelihood of Recovery?

Although there are treatments that effectively handle OCD symptoms, it remains a chronic disorder. Symptoms may disappear spontaneously or as a result of treatment; in fact, nine of every 10 individuals with OCD experience a waxing and waning of symptoms without remission, often only showing increases in symptoms when brought on by stress.[2] Individuals who no longer suffer symptoms, therefore, may not be entirely "recovered"; their symptoms may return at a time of great stress or in response to some biological or environmental changes. While most people experience a waxing and waning of symptoms, approximately 15 percent of OCD sufferers show progressive deterioration in social and occupational functioning.[1]

Although the general prognosis with no treatment is generally unfavorable, the suicide rate for individuals with OCD is lower than that for individuals with other psychiatric disorders.[4]

Documented recovery rates for individuals suffering from OCD are wide ranging. Estimates of the rate of spontaneous recovery from OCD range from 25 percent to 71 percent.[3] Individuals with OCD who receive either behavior therapy or a combination of medication and behavior therapy show the highest rate of recovery. Approximately 60 to 80 percent of clients who receive medications alone show moderate improvement in symptoms.[7] However, 70 to 90 percent of those treated with medication alone relapse within a few weeks after discontinuing use of the drug.[8]

Recovery rates may be more promising for those treated with behavior therapy. After completing behavior therapy, 80 to 90 percent of clients show noticeable improvement, and about 75 percent show long-term improvements in their OCD symptoms.[2] Although the majority of clients treated with behavior therapy show sustained improvement, about 20 percent relapse.[2] One drawback to using behavioral treatment, however, is that up to 25 percent of OCD sufferers refuse to participate or fail to complete this type of treatment because it requires facing fears to conquer them.[2] Therefore, the more accurate rate of recovery for behavior therapy lies somewhere around 60 percent, with 10 to 20 percent of those treated experiencing no significant reduction in symptoms.

Around 10 percent of individuals with OCD experience an episodic course with minimal or no symptoms between episodes. These episodes may last anywhere from several weeks to many months and usually become more severe over time.[2]

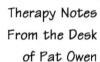

Therapy Notes
From the Desk
of Pat Owen

Saw Amy P. (age 36) today. Has a 10-year history of obsessions and compulsions. Includes irrational obsessive fears of hurting people, emotionally or physically; especially her family. Main rituals are repeating every-day actions to undo or neutralize cata-strophic ideas. Symptoms worse since baby born six months ago. Probably OCD, moderate severity. Check for comorbid depression.

Chapter Two: Diagnosing and Assessing Obsessive Compulsive Disorder

Diary of Amy P.

May 25

Saw Owen today. She asked a lot of questions and said she'd help me get things back under control, I think. I know I'm unreasonably worried about my family, so I've tried to stop doing everything over and over so much. It's all so depressing, and I'm so tired. Owen says I have to fill out this questionnaire called the "Padua." It has all these questions about how often I do things and how I think and feel. I hope this is worth all the trouble!

This chapter answers the following:

- **What Criteria are Used to Diagnose OCD?** — This section lists the DSM-IV diagnostic criteria.

- **What are the Typical Characteristics of Those with OCD?** — This section reviews the main identifying characteristics for OCD, including avoidance, experiencing guilt, overestimation harm, and worrying excessively.

- **What Tools are Available for Clinical Assessment?** — This section introduces clinical interviewing, self-report instruments, psychometric assessments, and physiological laboratory findings. Additional information can be found in Appendix A: Assessment Measures.

- **What Differentiates OCD from Other Disorders?** — This section provides information for differentiating OCD from other disorders.

What Criteria are Used to Diagnose OCD?

Because superstitions, rituals, or other behaviors can resemble OCD symptoms, correctly diagnosing OCD can be tricky. This chapter discusses how to differentiate between those behaviors and OCD as well as criteria used for diagnosis, typical characteristics of those with OCD, and tools available for clinical assessment.

The main criteria for diagnosing OCD comes from the leading psychiatric diagnostic manual used in the United States, the <u>Diagnostic and Statistical Manual of Mental Disorders, fourth edition</u>, published by the American Psychiatric Association.

DSM-IV Criteria

These are the DSM-IV criteria printed in the American Psychiatric Associations' *Diagnostic and Statistical Manual of Mental Disorders, Fourth Edition,* published in 1994.

A. Either obsessions or compulsions:

Obsessions as defined by (1), (2), (3), and (4):

1. recurrent and persistent thoughts, impulses, or images that are experienced, at some time during the disturbance, as intrusive and inappropriate and that cause marked anxiety or distress
2. the thoughts, impulses, or images are not simply excessive worries about real-life problems
3. the person attempts to ignore or suppress such thoughts, impulses or images, or to neutralize them with some other thought or action.
4. the person recognizes that the obsessional thoughts, impulses, or images are a product of his or her own mind (not imposed from without as in thought insertion)

Compulsions as defined by (1) and (2):

1. repetitive behaviors (e.g., hand washing, ordering, checking) or mental acts (e.g., praying, counting, repeating words silently) that the person feels driven to perform in response to an obsession, or according to rules that must be applied rigidly
2. the behaviors or mental acts are aimed at preventing or reducing distress or preventing some dreaded event or situation, however, these behaviors or mental acts either are not connected in a realistic way with what they are designed to neutralize or prevent or are clearly excessive

B. At some point during the course of the disorder, the person has recognized that the obsessions or compulsions are excessive or unreasonable. Note: This does not apply to children.

C. The obsessions or compulsions cause marked distress, are time consuming (take more than 1 hour a day), or significantly interfere with the person's normal routine, occupational (or academic) functioning, or usual social activities or relationships.

D. If another Axis I disorder is present, the content of the obsessions or compulsions is not restricted to it (e.g., preoccupation with food in the presence of an Eating Disorder; hair pulling in the presence of Trichotillomania; concern with appearance in the presence of Body Dysmorphic Disorder; preoccupation with

(Continued on Page 7)

(DSM-IV Criteria, Continued)

drugs in the presence of a Substance Use Disorder; preoccupation with having a serious illness in the presence of Hypochondriasis; preoccupation with sexual urges or fantasies in the presence of a Paraphilia; or guilty ruminations in the presence of Major Depressive Disorder.

E. The disturbance is not due to the direct physiological effects of a substance (e.g., a drug of abuse, a medication) or a general medical condition.

Specify if:

With Poor Insight: if, for most of the time during the current episode, the person does not recognize that the obsessions and compulsions are excessive or unreasonable

(Reprinted with permission by the American Psychiatric Association: Diagnostic and Statistical Manual of Mental Disorders, Fourth Edition. Washington DC, American Psychiatric Association, 1994)

What are Typical Characteristics of Those with OCD?

Those who suffer from OCD may have only a few or suffer from many typical symptoms. These symptoms distress the individual and often cause problems in the work place and in personal relationships. In rare instances, OCD may leave a person house-bound when sufferer's fears and worries make it easier to stay home in perceived relative safety rather than risk facing situations that may trigger their OCD. Typical symptoms experienced by those with OCD include:

- **Avoiding situations that involve the content of their obsessions.** For example, an individual with obsessions about dirt may avoid public lavatories or shaking hands with strangers. Extensively avoiding situations can result in extreme life-style changes.

- **Experiencing guilt and a pathological sense of responsibility.** Many fear that their thoughts might cause harm to others or make something terrible happen, because many individuals with OCD believe that having a thought is the same as actually acting on that thought. Further, many OCD sufferers perform compulsions because they believe that failing to "correct" a problem is equivalent to causing it. Their compulsions are a way of undoing or fixing something they fear they may have done wrong or something that might result in harm to others (e.g., removing a rock from the road so that a car does not subsequently hit it and have an accident).

- **Overestimating harm.** Another OCD characteristic is a tendency to overestimate both the likelihood of harm and the severity of the consequences.[9] OCD sufferers may assume that an environment is dangerous until proven safe. This contrasts sharply with a common presumption that all is well unless danger is obvious.

- **Worrying and ruminating excessively.** Anxious individuals may find themselves frequently thinking about personal and/or family concerns that may or may not be linked to obsessions. Such individuals may use *sedatives* excessively to try to combat their symptoms. They may also try to control their fears by using alcohol or *hypnotics*.

sedatives – *medications that help suppress anxiety by calming agitation and relaxing muscles*

hypnotics – *medications that promote sleep*

What Tools are Available for Clinical Assessment?

Clinical assessment involves gathering specific information from:

- Clinical interviews

- Self-report instruments and structured interviews

- Behavioral assessments

- Psychometric assessments

- Physiological laboratory findings

Clinical Interviews

During the clinical interview, the therapist gathers information about obsessive cues and rituals, medical history, individual and family psychiatric history, social and occupational functioning, the role of relatives, and client insight.

Obsessive Cues and Rituals

In addition to questions of history and current functioning, the interviewer inquires about:

- External sources of obsessive fear (e.g., seeing lights on, touching a doorknob, reading about AIDS, or hearing news about a hit-and-run accident)

- Internal cues, including thoughts, images, impulses, and feared consequences of not performing compulsions

- Avoidance behavior (e.g., not driving because of fear of running over a pedestrian).[7]

Medical History

A number of illnesses, lesions, or toxins can damage the brain structures related to OCD, thereby mimicking or causing OCD symptoms.[10-16] Therefore, the clinician can only diagnose OCD if a current medical evaluation indicates that the symptoms are not due to a General Medical Condition. This evaluation should include tests to rule out medical conditions that can cause excessive worry, nervousness, and other OCD-like symptoms, including:

- **Brain tumor or abnormal blood vessels**

- **Brain injury, infection or disease such as:**
  - Injury to brain, causing *Anoxia*
  - Toxic exposure (carbon monoxide poisoning or manganese intoxication)
  - Brain infection, such as viral *Encephalitis* that may result in *Post-Encephalitic Parkinsonism* or a bacterial infection that spread to the brain (*Sydenham's Chorea*).
  - Degenerative brain disease, such as Parkinson's disease, *Progressive Supranuclear Palsy*, Huntington's Chorea, Multiple Sclerosis, or Dementia.

- **General medical illnesses such as:**
  - Diabetes Mellitus
  - Thyroid impairment

If the client hasn't had a medical evaluation within the previous year, one should be arranged.

Anoxia – brain cell death resulting from interruption of oxygen supply to the brain

Encephalitis – infection of the brain

Post-Encephalitic Parkinsonism — rigidity, tremor, and abnormally slow movements that develop as a result of encephalitis lethargica or "sleeping sickness"

Sydenham's Chorea – condition triggered by rheumatic infection of the brain and characterized by involuntary, irregular muscle movements involving the face, neck, and limbs

Progressive Supranuclear Palsy – weakness and paralysis caused by brain cell deterioration in the cerebral cortex, basal ganglia, and other upper motor areas

For more information on distinguishing OCD from other disorders, see pages 15-20.

- **Substances or medications, such as:**
  - Amphetamines or stimulants
  - Cocaine or crack
  - Diet pills
  - Hallucinogens (LSD, "acid")

- **Developmental or Learning Problems, such as:**
  - Mental retardation
  - Autism

- **Other psychiatric conditions, such as:**
  - Depression
  - Other anxiety disorders, such as Panic Disorder, Generalized Anxiety Disorder, or Post Traumatic Stress Disorder
  - Psychotic disorders, such as delusional disorders or Schizophrenia

Individual and Family Psychiatric History

An individual psychiatric history needs to include questions on:

- The age of onset of OCD symptoms

- Severity and pattern of symptoms (episodic versus persistent)

- Significant stresses (psychosocial and medical)

- Evidence of depression, other psychiatric illness, or personality disorder

Schizotypal Personality Disorder – a personality disorder characterized by markedly eccentric and erratic thought, speech, and behavior and a tendency to withdraw from other people

These indicators help determine the prognosis and shape the treatment plan. For example, severe symptoms without an associated significant stressor and accompanied by evidence of *Schizotypal Personality Disorder* suggest a poor prognosis.[17] Such conditions may necessitate long-term therapy as well as drug interventions. On the other hand, mild symptoms, an identifiable significant stressor, and lack of a personality disorder, suggest a very favorable treatment outlook. Brief behavioral interventions may be sufficient for the symptoms to go into remission.

Family and genetic histories provide clues about OCD diagnosis. Client assessment and initial screening should include questions about family psychiatric history, especially the presence of *Tourette's Syndrome* in relatives, since Tourette's is more common in families of those with OCD.[1]

Tourette's Syndrome – neurological disorder characterized by semi-voluntary motor tics and vocalizations

Social and Occupational Functioning

Collecting a social and occupational history will help identify any functional impairment required to diagnose OCD. Ask about school or job performance, socializing, and status of friendships and intimate relationships. To diagnose OCD, obsessions and compulsions must consume at least one hour per day and cause marked distress or significant interference in a person's routine, occupational functioning, and/or usual social activities and relationships. Therefore, a clinician must determine if these criteria are met using questions, such as:

- How much time per day do you spend obsessing and ritualizing?

- Have your symptoms caused you much distress?

- Have your obsessions and compulsions interfered with your occupational or academic functioning, causing you to lose jobs or drop out of school?

- Have your symptoms interfered with your functioning in social or family situations?

- Have your symptoms caused marked distress in your social activities or relationships?

Based on the answers to these questions, the clinician first determines whether or not the criteria for OCD have been met. If so, the clinician assesses the severity and pervasiveness of the symptoms. The more severe the symptoms and the occupational and social impairment, the poorer the treatment *prognosis*. OCD sufferers with moderate symptoms and modest or relatively recent impairments in occupational and social functioning respond best to behavioral interventions.

prognosis– outcome in the future

Role of Relatives

Because family members' attitudes and responses have been found to predict treatment outcome, the clinician must determine the role of relatives. Those who are emotionally overinvolved or hostile to the client negatively influence the treatment outcome.[18] A recent study found that 75 percent of relatives of persons with OCD were participating at least minimally in rituals, avoidance, or modifying their own behavior to accommodate the clients' symptoms.[18] Family involvement in the client's rituals may interfere with successful treatment, making early identification of this obstacle essential. Family participation in the OCD sufferer's rituals is highly related to:

- Greater family dysfunction

- Family distress

- Rejection of the OCD client by family members

Client Insight

Those who perceive their obsessions and compulsions as irrational have a better treatment prognosis. According to changes in the DSM-IV, however, OCD may still be diagnosed even though the individual fails to recognize the irrationality of his or her obsessions or compulsions during episodes. DSM-IV designates these individuals as, "With Poor Insight."[1] However, DSM-IV does specify that adults with OCD must comprehend that their obsessions or compulsions are excessive or unreasonable at some point during the course of the disorder. Clients who have poor insight and overestimate the likelihood of harm are less likely to benefit from behavior therapy but may be helped by medications.[19] Most people with OCD know their fears and rituals are irrational between episodes; however, they may lose this insight in the face of their obsessional cues. These OCD sufferers are much more likely to benefit from behavior therapy and medications than those who are continually convinced of the accuracy of their obsessive fears.

Self-Report Instruments and Structured Interviews

There are two general classes of instruments used to detect and diagnose OCD. The first includes self-report instruments completed by clients to either screen for OCD in various settings or to classify subjects for research purposes. For example:

- Maudsley Obsessional Compulsive Inventory (MOCI)

- Padua Inventory (PI)

- Compulsive Activity Checklist (CAC)

- Yale-Brown Obsessive Compulsive Checklist and Scale (Y-BOCS) — Self-report version

The second class of instruments includes structured interviews in which trained clinicians follow a strict interview format to probe for OCD diagnosis and severity. These instruments include:

- Structured Clinical Interview for DSM-IV (SCID)

- Anxiety Disorders Interview Schedule (ADIS)

- Yale-Brown Obsessive Compulsive Scale (Y-BOCS) and Symptom Checklist — Interview Version

Appendix A covers these instruments in detail.

For specific information on these instruments, see appendix A on pages 81-85.

Behavior Assessment

Behavioral Avoidance Tests (BAT) were originally developed to measure fear and avoidance in people with phobias.[20] Several types of BATs have been used to assess obsessive-compulsive symptoms. A single-task BAT involves presenting the client with a feared stimulus, perhaps a garbage can. The therapist asks the client to approach as close as possible to the object and report his or her level of discomfort on a 100-point *Subjective Units of Distress* (*SUDs) scale*. The clinician measures avoidance behavior in terms of the SUDs scale and the client's distance from the feared object or willingness to engage in sequential exposure steps.

Subjective Units of Distress scale (SUDs) — a scale ranging from 10-100 with 10 being the least anxiety provoking and 100 being the most anxiety provoking. The SUDs scoring system allows the client to express exactly how upsetting or distressing certain stimuli are in comparison to other anxiety experiences.

Because a single-task BAT may fail to capture the range of an individual's obsessive-compulsive symptoms, multi-task BATs are needed for most OCD clients. In this approach, the clinician has clients repeat the avoidance test with several different objects or situations that represent the range of their fears. BATs provide "real-life" measures of fear and avoidance in OCD and are well suited for assessing fear and avoidance of "contaminated" stimuli associated with washing compulsions. However, BATs may be more difficult to apply in cases of checking, repeating, or ordering compulsions. Another problem with BATs is that a client's fear and avoidance may be situation-specific. The OCD sufferer may fear and avoid touching objects at home yet handle objects fearlessly in other environments. In these cases, conduct a BAT at home or in whatever environment symptoms emerge.

Psychometric Assessments

psychometric tests –
tests that measure
psychological factors,
such as personality,
intelligence, beliefs, fears

In inpatient and outpatient settings, clinicians regularly use *psychometric tests* to facilitate diagnosis and describe client personality characteristics. Although these instruments are not specific to OCD clients, they may provide clinicians with useful information. Commonly used psychometric instruments are:

- Minnesota Multiphasic Personality Inventories (MMPI and MMPI-2)

- Rorschach Inkblot Test

- Thematic Apperception Test (TAT)

- Wechsler Adult Intelligence Scale - Revised (WAIS-R)

For specific information
on these tests, refer to
appendix A on pages
86-88.

Appendix A covers these assessment measures in detail.

Physiological Laboratory Findings

Laboratory findings, although helpful in continued research regarding the cause or effects of OCD on human physiology, do not appear to add precision to diagnostic decisions. According to the DSM-IV, there are no laboratory findings specific to an OCD diagnosis.[1]

What Differentiates OCD from Other Disorders?

When diagnosing OCD, the therapist must rule out the possibility that the client's symptoms are related to:

- Addictive Disorders
- Anxiety Disorder Due to a General Medical Condition
- Body Dysmorphic Disorder or Specific/Social Phobia
- Delusional Disorder or Psychotic Disorder Not Otherwise Specified
- Generalized Anxiety Disorder, Panic Disorder, Agoraphobia, or Post Traumatic Stress Disorder
- Hypochondriasis or Somatization Disorder
- Major Depressive Episode or mood disorder
- Obsessive Compulsive Personality Disorder
- Schizophrenia
- Substance-Induced Anxiety Disorder
- Superstitions and Repetitive Checking Behaviors
- Tic Disorder or Tourette's Syndrome

Addictive Disorders

Although labeled "compulsive," addictive behaviors (e.g., excessive eating, sexual behavior, gambling, or substance use) are unlike OCD compulsions. People performing impulsive behaviors, such as gambling, usually derive pleasure from the activity. They wish to resist it only because of harmful consequences, such as losing all their money. In contrast, individuals with OCD perform compulsions to reduce anxiety by avoiding some imagined negative consequence (e.g., someone having an accident or a house burning down).

People with OCD do not enjoy participating in their compulsions. They would gladly give up these behaviors if they did not have to experience the anxiety that happens whenever they try to stop the rituals.

Anxiety Disorder Due to a General Medical Condition

To ensure appropriate treatment, the clinician needs to determine if the anxiety or obsessive compulsive symptoms are related to or caused by a primary medical condition. A physician can use medical history, laboratory findings, or physical examination to rule out that possibility.[1] General medical conditions that may cause anxiety include:

- **Endocrine problems, such as:**

  - Hyperthyroidism
  - Hypothyroidism
  - Pheochromocytoma
  - Hypoglycemia or Hyperglycemia (diabetes)

- **Cardiac problems, such as:**

  - Heart failure
  - Arrhythmia (irregular heart beat)

- **Pulmonary problems, such as:**

  - Chronic obstructive pulmonary disease (emphysema, asthma)
  - Embolism
  - Pneumonia
  - Hyperventilation

- **Nutritional problems, such as:**

  - Vitamin B12 deficiency
  - Porphyria

- **Other conditions** (see pages 9-10)

  - Neoplasms (tumors, cancer)
  - Encephalitis

Body Dysmorphic Disorder and Specific/Social Phobias

Social Phobia – a disorder characterized by episodes of panic anxiety in social settings, due to excessive concern about public embarrassment or possible adverse scrutiny

Recurrent or intrusive thoughts, images, or behaviors often occur in the context of other mental disorders. The clinician should not diagnose OCD if the content of the client's thoughts or activities is exclusively related to another mental disorder. For instance, a preoccupation with appearance accompanied by an irrational fear of having a physical defect, and related checking rituals would be diagnosed as Body Dysmorphic Disorder. Similarly, a preoccupation limited to a feared object (e.g., snakes), or situation would be diagnosed as a Specific or *Social Phobia*. An additional diagnosis of OCD may be warranted if there are obsessions or compulsions whose content is not related to the other mental disorder.

Delusional Disorder or Psychotic Disorder

A person's ability to realize that obsessions or compulsions are excessive or irrational occurs on a continuum. In some individuals with OCD, reality testing may be absent, and the obsession may reach delusional proportions (e.g., actually believing that one caused a plane to crash by having willed it). In such cases, the presence of psychotic features may warrant an additional diagnosis of Delusional Disorder or Psychotic Disorder Not Otherwise Specified. The specifier, "With Poor Insight," may be helpful in situations that are on the boundary between obsession and delusion. For example, an OCD sufferer who realizes most of the time that they are not responsible for plane crashes but occasionally worries that they really might have caused one, would be diagnosed as having OCD with poor insight.

OCD can be diagnosed concurrently with a Psychotic Disorder when criteria for both disorders are met.

Schizophrenia

Like some schizophrenic delusions, the content of OCD obsessions may be quite bizarre, such as the belief that one might accidentally seal one's self into an envelope and get deposited into a mailbox.[2] The difference is that OCD sufferers are aware of the irrational nature of these fears. They typically do not show other symptoms of psychosis or schizophrenia, such as:

- Marked *loosening of associations*
- Prominent *hallucinations*
- Grossly *inappropriate affect*
- *Thought insertion*

loosening of associations – an individual's speech slips off the track from one topic to another

hallucinations – false sensory perceptions

inappropriate affect – mood incongruent with context of a situation

thought insertion – the belief that some other being is placing thoughts in one's mind

Generalized Anxiety Disorder, Panic Disorder, Agoraphobia, or Post-Traumatic Stress Disorder

The worries experienced by those with **Generalized Anxiety Disorder (GAD)** are excessive and persistent concerns about real-life circumstances. In contrast, those with OCD experience obsessions whose content is more likely to be unrealistic and seen by the client as inappropriate.[2] For example, persistent but fairly rational worries about finances, health concerns, or one's job would be considered GAD, whereas irrational fears of causing a fire by leaving the stove on or harming one's child with a knife constitute obsessions.

The presence of rituals is unique to OCD. For example, a person with GAD may worry constantly about having enough money to pay their bills. However, they will not engage in behaviors, such as repetitively counting their money or excessively calling the bank to check on their deposits.

The hallmark of **Panic Disorder** is the presence of spontaneous, unprovoked panic attacks. While certain thoughts or stimuli (e.g., germs), can precipitate anxiety attacks that resemble panic in OCD, OCD sufferers do not experience unprovoked anxiety. Instead, intrusive images or certain stimuli trigger anxiety in OCD.

Agoraphobia is characterized by a fear of crowds. OCD sufferers can also avoid crowds, but this response is due to a fear of contamination or acting on unwanted or aggressive impulses. In contrast, people with agoraphobia avoid crowds due to concerns about becoming trapped or not being able to escape.

Recurrent images or flashbacks can occur during **Post-Traumatic Stress Disorder (PTSD)**, but these symptoms emerge after a life-threatening event or tragedy that has already occurred. In OCD, the intrusive thoughts or excessive fears concern things that <u>might</u> happen.

Hypochondriasis/Somatization Disorder

Hypochondriasis should be diagnosed instead of OCD if persistent, distressing thoughts are exclusively related to fears of a serious illness despite considerable evidence (reassurances from physicians, normal test results, etc.) to the contrary. While individuals with OCD may worry about and seek medical help for multiple, presumed physical symptoms or diseases, they realize their concerns are excessive. However, if the concern about having a disease is focused on one medical condition (such as cancer) and is followed by rituals, such as excessive washing or checking the body, then OCD may be considered as an alternative diagnosis or added as a secondary diagnosis to Hypochondriasis.

Major Depressive Episode

Ruminations are common in depressed individuals and develop as part of a depressed mood. They tend to resolve with effective treatment of the depression. Unlike individuals with OCD who attempt to ignore or suppress obsessions, people with depression do not typically try to suppress or ignore their depressive brooding.[2]

Both OCD and Major Depression often involve symptoms of isolation and sleep disturbance. However, it is the source of these disturbances, rather than the disturbance itself, that differentiates depression from OCD. For example, a sleep disturbance caused by obsessional worry that one has caused a catastrophe would be related to OCD, while sleep disturbance accompanied by a sense of despair and hopelessness would signify depression.

Obsessive-Compulsive Personality Disorder

Although the names, "OCD" and "Obsessive-Compulsive Personality Disorder (OCPD)" are similar, the clinical presentations of the two are quite different. OCPD does not involve the presence of true obsessions or compulsions. Instead, it involves a pervasive pattern of preoccupation with orderliness, perfectionism, rigid rules, and control at the expense of flexibility and openness. Individuals with OCPD do not clean or check things because they fear a tragedy may result. Rather, they simply require order, perfection, and control in their lives. Hoarding or excessive collecting of possessions can be a symptom of OCPD or OCD. If an individual expresses symptoms of both disorders, the clinician can make a dual diagnosis.

Substance-Induced Anxiety Disorder

Substance-Induced Anxiety Disorder is new to DSM-IV. Its diagnosis involves excessive anxiety judged by the clinician to be directly related to the physiological effect of a substance (e.g, abusing a medication or an illicit drug, the side effects of a prescribed or over-the-counter medication, or exposure to a toxin). To differentiate Substance-Induced Anxiety Disorder from OCD, determine by a careful history and perhaps a urine drug screen whether the use of or cessation from an illicit substance, alcohol, or a medication triggered the obsessions or compulsions.[1]

Superstitions and Repetitive Checking Behaviors

Superstitious behaviors, although frequently encountered in everyday life, lead to a diagnosis of OCD only if these behaviors are:

Major Depressive Episode and OCD occur concurrently in 30 to 35 percent of people with OCD seeking treatment. If all other criteria for OCD are met, symptoms of sleep disturbance, isolation, and brooding resulting from obsessions and compulsions would indicate an OCD diagnosis rather than a Major Depressive Episode.

People with OCPD do not usually complain of anxiety.

Symptoms of Substance-Induced Anxiety Disorder may be found from either use or cessation of both prescription and nonprescription drugs.

- Elaborated repetitively

- Appear to have obsessive content (e.g., magical thinking that triggers rituals, consuming more than one hour of time per day).

- Result in clinically significant impairment or distress

Tic Disorder

In contrast to compulsions, tics are sudden, rapid, recurrent, nonrhythmic, stereotyped motor movements or vocalizations (e.g., eye blinking, tongue protrusion, or throat clearing), which are often performed in response to sensations of subjective discomfort. Tics are not aimed at neutralizing an obsession or preventing an unwanted outcome. Some people have both OCD and a Tic Disorder (especially Tourette's Disorder).

Therapy Notes
From the Desk
of Pat Owen

Met with Amy P. today. No recent medical evaluation, so scheduled one. OCD diagnosis is clear. Continues to repeat actions and even thoughts obsessively, well over one hour a day. Definitely interferes with interpersonal relationships, now beginning to affect relationship with husband.

Staying home more and more to avoid seeing things (devil symbols, occult signs, bad numbers, etc.) that trigger obsessions. Avoids newspapers and television also. Y-BOCS score = 32, very high. Depression is worrisome, some suicidal thoughts. Start SRI antidepressant medication, if feasible.

Chapter Three: Environmental Treatments for Obsessive Compulsive Disorder

---

Diary of Amy P.

June 6

Saw Owen again. She recommended medication for my depression first. I sure feel down — I'll try anything. She said that even low doses of these SRI drugs might help both my depression and my OCD. Good thing I stopped breast feeding a month ago.

Jim's getting tired of my crazy stuff, and I can't blame him. Owen wants to talk to both of us together about behavior therapy. It scares me, but I've got to do something. She says I might feel less afraid if my depression improves.

This chapter answers the following:

● **What are the Environmental Influences that may cause OCD?** — *This section presents various theoretical approaches to understanding OCD from a psychological perspective. These include behavioral, cognitive, and psychoanalytic theories as well as group and family therapy approaches.*

● **What Psychological Interventions are Used to Treat OCD?** — *Treatment methods follow the theoretical discussion for each of the approaches listed in the previous section.*

● **How Effective are Psychological Treatments for OCD?** — *The final section of each treatment method reviews research on the effectiveness of that particular approach.*

etiology — the cause of a disorder

For decades, researchers have searched for the origin of OCD. Unfortunately, while successful treatments suggest possible causes of OCD, the exact *etiology* remains unknown. Because both psychological and biological treatment studies indicate similar results and because combining these treatments is effective, some researchers suggest that questioning whether or not OCD has a single origin is outdated.[17] The most accurate answer to the question of OCD's etiology is that psychological, biological, and environmental factors are involved in the disorder's etiology.

Recent research indicates that both behavioral and medication treatments produce similar beneficial changes in brain function; demonstrating that the psychology and biology of OCD are interrelated. This research indicates that successful behavior therapy results in similar changes or adaptions in the underlying function of certain brain areas that occur after effective medication therapy. Specifically, after 10 weeks of treatment with behavior therapy or *serotonergic medication*, approximately the same number of clients improved in both groups. In the improved clients, no matter what method of treatment was used, the previously hyperactive areas in the brain returned to normal. Though the treatments seem very different, they may ultimately achieve success through the same mechanisms.[21, 22]

This chapter explores environmental influences that may cause OCD and reviews corresponding psychological interventions. Chapter 4 explores biological theories, including the *serotonin hypothesis*, that suggest that certain brain regions and the underlying transmission of the neurotransmitter serotonin may cause or mediate OCD symptoms. Chapter 4 also explores in detail the effectiveness of using medications and psychotherapy individually and in combination.

What Environmental Influences May Cause OCD?

Many theorists believe that environment and life experiences play a major role in OCD's origin. There are numerous theories regarding the environmental causes and individual treatments of OCD. This section examines the following:

- **Behavioral Theories and Treatments.** These theories emphasize a learned pattern of fear and avoidance behavior in response to a certain stimulus or situation. For example, an individual may refuse to use public lavatories due to an intense fear of being contaminated by germs. The behavioral model focuses on how individuals acquire obsessions by learning to associate a neutral event with fear. The individual then attempts to cope with that fear or anxiety by performing compulsive rituals reinforced because they temporarily reduce this anxiety. Behavioral treatments are based on *habituation* of anxiety and/or distress when the client confronts feared situations.

---

serotonergic medication — medications that specifically effect the neurotransmitter serotonin

serotonin hypothesis — the theory that impaired serotonin neurotransmission in the brain is related to OCD development

The multidimensional nature of OCD's origin has brought about distinct treatment models. These models are based on theories that specifically focus on psychological origins as well as those theories suggesting a neurophysiological origin.

See pages 24-30 for a complete discussion of behavioral treatment methods.

habituation — gradual, naturally occurring reduction of anxiety or discomfort over time, if exposure is maintained

• **Cognitive Theories and Treatments.** These theories propose that expectations and beliefs about threat, control, and responsibility influence anxious responses to previously neutral stimuli. For example, an individual may feel responsible for an intrusive thought about harming others impulsively and thus may repeatedly check while driving to be sure he or she has not hit a pedestrian. Cognitive models focus on how an individual's perceptions, internal thoughts, images, and belief systems affect behavior when experiencing an intrusive (obsessive) idea. Treatment methods employ techniques to promote rational thinking and tend to incorporate behavioral strategies because of the interplay between cognitions and behavior.

See pages 33-40 for a complete discussion of cognitive treatment methods.

• **Psychoanalytic Theories and Treatments.** The Psychoanalytic model assumes that both personal history and early development interact to determine:

— An individual's personality
— Coping styles that may increase vulnerability for psychological problems, such as OCD.

See pages 40-45 for a complete discussion of psychoanalytic treatment methods.

Treatment methods focus on identifying early life events and family relationships affecting present emotions and behavior that contribute to OCD symptoms.

• **Group and Family Treatments.** Group and family therapies focus on the interpersonal aspects of the development of and the improvement in OCD symptoms. These treatments are based mainly on behavioral methods using group and family assistants to encourage client cooperation.

See pages 45-55 for a complete discussion of group and Family treatment methods.

What is the Behavioral Therapy Approach to Treating OCD?

In general, behavioral theory and treatment focus on how behavior is learned and how it can be unlearned. Treatment models for behavioral therapy stem from a two-stage theory for the acquisition and maintenance of fear and avoidance behavior.[2] According to this theory, a neutral object, (e.g., a knife or toilet) or thought (e.g., an image of the devil or the number "13") first becomes associated with fear by being paired with an anxiety-provoking stimulus (e.g., fear of contamination or an image of harming someone else). To reduce the anxiety developed, clients use escape or avoidance responses that are repeated and reinforced because they initially decrease anxiety.

Behavioral therapists believe that obsessions give rise to anxiety, and compulsions temporarily reduce that anxiety.[2] Individuals with OCD use compulsive rituals to actively reduce distress because what triggers obsessions is so prominent that it cannot be passively avoided. For example, an individual washes his or her hands dozens of times daily because he or she cannot avoid dirt and germs entirely.

What Treatment Methods are Used with a Behavioral Approach?

Based on the theory that obsessions evoke anxiety or discomfort, which is then reduced by compulsions, early behavioral theorists believed that OCD treatment should include anxiety-reducing procedures and a way to block the reinforcement embedded in the emission of rituals. This section reviews these early behavioral treatments, which led to the more current treatment methods: Imagined Exposure, In-vivo Exposure, and Response Prevention. This section also addresses common concerns about Exposure and Response Prevention and presents research on the effectiveness of behavioral treatments with OCD.

Early Behavioral Treatments

Early behavioral treatments focused on reducing the anxiety associated with obsessions. Practitioners believed that once obsessional cues ceased to evoke anxiety, compulsive behavior would stop because it was no longer reinforced by its anxiety-reducing properties. For example, once a person no longer felt so anxious at the thought of being contaminated, he or she would reduce or stop excessive cleaning rituals. Clinicians expected these anxiety-reducing treatments to make the client more comfortable in anxiety-eliciting situations by using prolonged exposure. This mental or physical exposure also breaks the connection between the anxiety-producing stimulus and feared disaster because exposure fails to result in disaster. Clients' expectations of negative consequences are not reinforced, and they adopt new, more rational expectations when faced with the previously anxiety-producing situation. Some of the early anxiety-reducing treatments for OCD, most of which proved to be of little help, included:[23]

- *Systematic Desensitization.* This procedure consists of inducing a state of relaxation in the client and then presenting anxiety-evoking items arranged in a hierarchical order. Clinicians believed that the pairing of relaxation with the disturbing stimuli would wear down (habituate) associated anxiety.

  systematic desensitization — a clinical technique that pairs relaxation with imagery of anxiety-eliciting situations

- *Paradoxical Intention.* This treatment involves deliberate attempts to increase the frequency or intensity of obsessions or compulsions to reduce discomfort.[21] For example, a therapist asks a client to deliberately think about germs and needing to wash more than usual because the danger from germs is so great. The therapist then assigns homework based on this scenario.

  paradoxical intention — a technique where the therapist instructs the client to do more of the obsessions or compulsions

- *Imagined Flooding.* Imagined Flooding usually involves the therapist encouraging the client to mentally experience their fears during the therapy session. For example, a client who compulsively checks things might be asked to visualize leaving the house without checking any locks and experiencing what that would feel like. The therapist might also ask the client to visualize a feared outcome, such as being robbed.

  imagined flooding — a clinical procedure where the therapist helps the client repeatedly visualize being exposed to a certain obsessive cue without ritualizing until that cue or situation no longer evokes anxiety or discomfort

- *Satiation.* Satiation focuses on verbal repetition. For example, a client fearful that repeating certain words or phrases would lead to his mother's death might be asked to repeatedly discuss those fears in great detail with the help of the therapist. The verbalized obsession might also be tape recorded for playback as homework.

  satiation — a clinical procedure where the therapist has the client verbalize ruminations while the therapist encourages the client through the use of verbal prompts

Aversion Relief — the process of punishing behavior followed by the ending of the punishment when the person stopped thinking the undesired thoughts or displaying undesired behaviors.

Thought Stopping — disrupting thoughts by having the person use the word or image "Stop!" immediately following the thought to be prevented.

Additional early behavioral treatments, such as *Aversion Relief* and *Thought Stopping* were aimed at blocking obsessions and compulsions.

Aversion Relief involved the act of punishing an undesired behavior or ritual and stopping the punishment when the undesired behavior stopped. For example, a therapist might make electric shock contingent on doing a ritual, such as hand washing. The therapist would then stop the shock as soon as the person touched a contaminated object. Therefore, clients experienced discomfort when they performed a ritual and relief when they touched feared objects, the reverse of their usual pattern. This method can also be applied to mental rituals so that the person experiences relief when no longer engaging in obsessive thoughts. In effect, the shock reciprocally inhibits the problematic rituals due to its aversive nature. This treatment is intended to teach the client to resist rituals even in the face of obsession-eliciting stimuli.[23]

The process of **Thought Stopping** aims to prohibit obsessions by replacing them with more pleasant and calming thoughts. It involves disrupting obsessional thoughts through the use of a cue word, like "Stop!" The therapist teaches the client to utilize this cue word when experiencing unwanted obsessional thoughts. In addition, the therapist instructs the client to visualize a pleasant scene immediately after saying the cue word. For example, a therapist would teach an individual who always fears hitting someone while driving to say, "Stop!" when the thought that he or she has hit someone arises. Immediately after saying "Stop," the client pictures a happy and pleasant scene. The client decides what scene to imagine (e.g., a sunny day on a tropical beach or a beautiful cabin on a lake in the mountains).

These early behavioral treatments for OCD included some form of exposure to obsessive material. However, rituals were often not included in treatment, and this may be why most of these approaches proved only partially effective in OCD treatment. Currently, the far more successful behavioral treatment of Exposure and Response Prevention incorporates the more helpful aspects of these early interventions, such as exposure to the feared stimuli.

Exposure and Response Prevention

Currently the most effective psychological treatment for OCD is *Exposure and Response Prevention*. This therapy employs prolonged Exposure to obsessional cues and prevention of compulsive rituals.[24] Exposure and Response Prevention consists of two main components, that is *In-vivo or Imagined Exposure* followed by *Response Prevention*.

In-vivo and/or Imagined Exposure elicit anxiety in the client for periods of one to two hours. Then, the clinician asks the client to refrain from performing any compulsions while anxiety levels decrease. Response Prevention is always included in Imagined Exposure scenes and always follows Exposure In-vivo. These treatment methods are described in step-by-step fashion by Steketee in the book, <u>Treatment of Obsessive Compulsive Disorder</u> and summarized below.[17]

- **In-vivo Exposure.** Exposure In-vivo consists of approximately one to two hours of actual confrontation with the feared stimulus; however, relaxation techniques are not utilized because they have not proved helpful and are unlikely to be useful when clients are experiencing high levels of anxiety or discomfort.[23] In initial consultations with the clinician, each client determines a hierarchy of feared situations from low anxiety-producing situations to extreme anxiety-producing situations. Based on this hierarchy, anxiety-evoking objects or situations are introduced to the client in a gradual or hierarchical manner, starting with items that evoke moderate discomfort. The clinician presents each object or situation in the hierarchy until the client experiences significantly less anxiety or distress. At this point, treatment proceeds to the next Exposure item on the hierarchy.

  With many obsessions, In-vivo Exposure in the clinician's office is not feasible. For example, one could not replicate in an office a client's obsessive thoughts that he or she just hit someone on the road with a car. However, a number of cleaning, checking, and counting obsessions are amenable to In-vivo Exposure in the therapist's office. For an obsessive cleaner, a clinician might present small quantities of dirt or some other

Exposure and Response Prevention (therapy) — the client confronts obsessional cues and is prevented from performing compulsions

In-vivo Exposure — exposure to the actual anxiety-eliciting stimulus, such as a garbage can

Imagined Exposure — exposure to the feared stimuli through the use of mental imagery

Response Prevention — deliberate blocking of overt and mental rituals and obsessive avoidance behaviors

Recommended readings, therapy manuals, and self-help guides, listed in appendix B, assist clients and family members in understanding OCD and carrying out Exposure and Response Prevention.

contaminant and ask the client to run his or her hands through it and rub it on the face, hair, and clothes. For a compulsive counter, a clinician might require the client to take 13 steps or perform some action involving an anxiety-provoking number.

A technique that may be useful during In-vivo Exposure is *modeling*. In participant modeling, the clinician first demonstrates the desired behavior by making contact with the feared object, and then asks the client to do the same. Modeling may also be passive. In this case, the clinician performs the target behavior while asking the client to closely observe these actions. In contrast to participant modeling, the clinician does not request that the client perform the behaviors. Passive modeling may achieve some symptom reduction but is inferior to participant modeling.[25]

modeling — the therapist demonstrates exposure for the client.

- **Imagined Exposure.** Imagined Exposure is used whenever In-vivo Exposure is impossible (e.g., with fear of a coworker dying of a heart attack or a son injured by a car.) The clinician presents the client with a series of scenes, (usually between four and 10), in increasing order of difficulty based on their hierarchical list of feared situations. This presentation starts with the least-feared scene and ends with the most-feared one. To induce the client into each feared situation, the clinician describes the event, object, or situation, including many sensory details, until the client has a clear picture of that stimulus context in mind. For example, with a compulsive checker, the clinician may describe a scene where the client imagines he or she has failed to check the stove properly, and the house catches fire. The clinician describes the situation, the client's actions, and the possible adverse consequences that the client fears may arise from the failure to check.

The clinician presents each scene continuously or repeats it several times until the client experiences considerably less anxiety or distress in response to that stimulus. The time required to complete a situation varies greatly between clients. Therapy sessions usually last between one and two hours, so it is sometimes necessary to use more than one session to complete one scene. At that point, the clinician presents the next scene in the hierarchy, continuing on until the client can experience all scenes without increased anxiety or distress.

Imagined Exposure differs from Systematic Desensitization in two ways:

1. Instead of being paired with relaxation, Exposure scenes are intended to elicit at least moderate levels of anxiety from the client. This anxiety shows habituation or reduction over time.

2. All scenes include Response Prevention so the client does not imagine performing compulsions.

- **Response Prevention.** Response Prevention involves prohibiting the ritualistic behavior either during or between therapy sessions for prolonged periods of several hours to days. Response Prevention is self-imposed by the client; it is never enforced by the clinician or anyone else with the use of physical restraint. During the therapy session, the clinician explains the importance of Response Prevention and describes feelings the client will likely experience. At home, a friend or relative often plays the role of the supporter, encouraging the client during the self-imposed Response Prevention to the feared objects or situations. Response Prevention is essentially the same regardless of the compulsion being prohibited. It simply involves the client waiting for long periods after Exposure to a feared situation, such as a garbage can, without performing any compulsive rituals like hand washing or showering to alleviate the anxiety. Compulsive urges gradually decline. Usually, the rituals are never permitted at all after Exposure; although, in some cases, a brief ritual may be allowed if circumstances require.

Behavior therapy is something the client has to do themselves. Thus, the clinician acts much like a training coach, designing workouts (homework assignments) that become progressively more difficult.

Most Exposure and Response Prevention occurs outside of therapy sessions due to expense and time constraints. The combination of Exposure and Response Prevention as a therapy program does not easily fit the typical, 50-minute therapy session. Some exposures can be accomplished in the clinician's office; however, most require the client to self-administer the therapy with the help of a support person between scheduled therapy sessions. Clients can designate a friend or relative to be this support person, having them remind the client of the rationale and instructions for using Response Prevention. Neither support persons nor clinicians may force the clients to do anything against their will.

The clinician requires the client to keep accurate records of self-imposed response prevention to facilitate follow-up at the next session.

Even though the clinician and helper encourage Response Prevention, compliance is ultimately up to the client.

People who comply with behavioral treatments do so despite the induced anxiety because they believe the long-term benefits outweigh the short-term discomfort.

Some people with OCD may prefer self-directed Exposure and Response Prevention, using one of the self-help treatment manuals listed on page 90. Some research indicates that for people with milder cases of OCD, self-exposure and self-imposed ritual prevention are as effective as Exposure and Response Prevention guided by a clinician.[26] Additionally, computerized exposure treatment programs are currently under investigation for their utility in treating OCD.[27, 28]

The process of response prevention differs for various clients, depending on their compulsive rituals. Long exposure periods have been found to be more effective than brief, interrupted exposures.[2] The exposure must not be terminated while the client's distress or anxiety level remains high, usually at least 30 minutes. Therefore, exposure sessions should last at least 45 minutes.[2] The optimum frequency of exposure sessions has not been studied, but clinical observation suggests that frequent or daily sessions are preferable in severe cases, though two to three sessions per week may be sufficient in moderate cases. When self-exposure homework between treatment sessions can be assessed, the clinician may be able to use weekly sessions with periodic telephone contacts to check on homework progress.

Exposure and Response Prevention is not indicated for individuals who are seriously depressed, delusional, or those who undermine therapy with overt or covert rituals, or avoidance techniques, as they are most likely to respond poorly to behavior therapy.[2, 8, 29] Additionally, OCD sufferers, convinced that obsessive worries or repetitive behaviors are realistic or rational, are less likely to respond to behavioral techniques. For those clients, biological treatments (reviewed in the next chapter) may enable them to respond better to behavior therapy.

How Effective is the Behavioral Therapy Approach in Treating OCD?

Of those who commit themselves to behavior therapy, less than 10 percent fail to complete it.

Approximately 25 percent of OCD clients refuse to participate in behavior therapy. However, those who faithfully expose themselves and remain in contact with anxiety-evoking situations without performing rituals until their anxiety lessens have pronounced reductions of rituals and discomfort associated with their obsessions.[30]

The research reviewed below covers:

- Initial OCD behavioral treatments

- More effective treatments using Exposure and Response Prevention

- Variations in Exposure and Response Prevention, including presentation of stimuli in treatment, level of supervision for treatment, and the treatment of mental rituals.

Initial OCD Behavioral Treatments

Early behavioral treatments, such as Systematic Desensitization, Satiation, and Paradoxical Intention are not as effective in treating OCD as current methods. Initially, Systematic Desensitization was reported as rather effective. However, later case reports indicated that it reduced symptoms in only 30 to 40 percent of clients and often required many treatment sessions.[23, 31, 32] Systematic Desensitization was found to be more effective when:

- Combined with In-vivo Exposure; exposure to the actual feared stimuli produced change in 60 percent of clients.

- There was a recent onset of symptoms rather than when used with individuals experiencing chronic OCD.

However, the effectiveness of Systematic Desensitization is questionable because these findings are based on small numbers of case reports. *Controlled research studies* on larger populations are needed to establish Systematic Desensitization as a viable treatment alternative for OCD. As a whole,

controlled research studies — research studies in which the various treatments in the study are regulated so that causal factors can be unambiguously identified

Paradoxical Intention, Satiation, Aversion Relief, and Thought Stopping are only partially successful in the treatment of OCD. [2]

Exposure and Response Prevention

Studies have shown that Imagined Exposure alone for OCD is an ineffective treatment. However, when combined with In-vivo Exposure, Imagined Exposure helps maintain the gains achieved with In-vivo Exposure.[17] *Meta-analyses* of Exposure and Response Prevention controlled-outcome studies indicate that the combination of Exposure and Response Prevention was highly successful in reducing obsessions and compulsions.[33, 34] This treatment yielded at least a 70 percent reduction in obsessions and rituals in 51 percent of those who completed a course of treatment. In addition, 39 percent of the clients had a 30 to 69 percent reduction in obsessions and rituals. In other words, 90 percent of the individuals with OCD who complied with Exposure and Response Prevention experienced moderate improvement, were much improved, or "recovered" by the end of treatment.

meta-analysis — *a study of the collective findings of many individual outcome studies to give an overall level of effectiveness for a certain type of treatment*

An additional published overview of OCD behavioral therapy outcome studies confirmed that between 80 and 90 percent of clients treated were classified as improved, with up to 80 percent reduction in symptom severity.[8] Even with dropouts and those who refuse treatment included, 63 percent of OCD clients achieved some symptom improvement from behavior therapy.[8]

Study results also indicate that approximately 70 to 80 percent of OCD clients treated with this procedure remained improved at follow-up, though follow-up times varied among studies.[8, 25] Several factors, though controversial, have been linked with a positive treatment outcome. These factors include early onset of symptoms and lower levels of pretreatment anxiety and depressed mood. On the other hand, symptom duration was not found to correlate with treatment outcome.[8, 17] Other factors affecting this therapy include:

- **Level of Supervision.** The clinician's supervision during Exposure and Response Prevention appears insignificant for outcome effect.[2] Treatment is equally successful regardless of clinician involvement. Further, clients engaging in self-directed Exposure and Response

Prevention therapy following treatment guidelines in a book show modest improvement.[35] Although limited, research results appear to indicate self-imposed Response Prevention is just as effective as Response Prevention under 24-hour supervision.[26] However, slightly better results have been achieved in the studies with strict Response Prevention.[2, 17]

- **Presentation of Stimuli.** With most clients, it does not matter if anxiety-provoking stimuli are presented hierarchically, beginning with the least distressing, or whether the most distressing stimulus is presented at treatment outset.[36] However, clinical observations suggest that clients are more receptive to a treatment program that gradually approaches their most-feared situations.[2]

- **Mental Rituals.** These are more difficult to treat than overt behavioral rituals because they are harder to identify and cannot be observed by the clinician. Therefore, behavioral treatment of individuals with mental rather than behavioral rituals has not been generally as successful. Clients who have mental compulsions have less control over their occurrence because, unlike active behaviors, there is little time or distinction between the urge to perform mental rituals and their actual performance.[2] However, the addition of cognitive therapy techniques to behavior therapy (that specifically targets mental rituals) appears to be very helpful in treating mental rituals.[37]

What is the Cognitive Therapy Approach to Treating OCD?

Cognitive theorists believe that people with OCD have impairment in their ability to organize and integrate information. They may respond to and process emotional cues with greater difficulty and discomfort, and they may misinterpret intrusive thoughts so that these become obsessions. This section reviews:

- Cognitive theories related to OCD

- Cognitive treatment strategies

- Efficacy research for using Cognitive Therapy with OCD

One cognitive explanation of OCD suggests that individuals suffer from the disorder because they have unusually high expectations of negative outcomes (e.g., believing they will die from touching a garbage can). In addition, they overestimate the negative consequences for a variety of actions (e.g., believing they have hit someone with their car when they have simply hit a pot hole or driven over a bump in the road).[2] Obsessional content typically involves exaggerations of normal concerns (e.g., health, death, welfare of others, sex, and religion).

Cognitive theorists believe that people with OCD suffer from some common *irrational beliefs* associated with obsessive fears.[38] These beliefs include:

irrational beliefs — *false perceptions of reality based on exaggerated expectations*

- Having a thought about doing an action is the same as performing the action.

- Not trying to prevent harm to self or others is the same as having caused the harm in the first place.

- Being personally responsible for thoughts or actions remains unchanged by other factors, such as a low probability that an event may occur or that others have a role in event outcomes.

- Failing to correct or undo an aggressive or violent thought equates to seeking or wanting such harm to actually happen.

- Exercising control over one's thoughts is mandatory.

- Being especially vigilant prevents disasters.

- Being absolutely certain that no harm has or will occur is important.

- Not performing perfectly is the same as failing.

Some cognitive theorists believe that normal intrusive thoughts may turn to obsessions when the person interprets or appraises the intrusion as potentially harmful and takes responsibility for causing this harm.[39, 40, 41] This appraisal leads to increased anxiety and guilt. The individual then develops avoidance behaviors and overt or covert compulsions to reduce the anxiety. The key element in this view of OCD is the negative automatic thoughts or interpretations that accompany intrusive experiences.[38] These thoughts may include, "Did I forget to check the stove and oven? I can't take the chance, or my house is going to burn down," or "Thinking about an accident makes me responsible for preventing it."

Another cognitive explanation for people with OCD is that they hold very basic erroneous beliefs, such as, "One must be completely competent in all endeavors to be worthwhile; therefore, I can't make any mistakes."[42] These erroneous beliefs lead to perfectionist striving that then provokes anxiety. Additionally, OCD sufferers may believe they cannot tolerate the anxiety and therefore devalue their ability to adequately deal with such threats. This dysfunctional cycle continues when individuals with OCD doubt that they can cope with the possibility of negative outcomes. Cognitive theorists view compulsions, such as "I must turn the car around and check to be sure I did not hit someone," as attempts to reduce the overestimated harm and excessive sense of responsibility they feel.

OCD reflects an impairment, not in the content, but in the organization and integration of thinking.[9] OCD seems to involve memory deficits or at least a lack of confidence in memory. OCD sufferers perceive information correctly; however, many have difficulties interpreting and making use of that information. Individuals with OCD repeatedly perform their compulsive rituals because they are not convinced that they have adequately processed information about threat. For example, an individual will check the car lights again and again, forgetting or doubting that they were already checked. Similarly, a man may turn his car around repeatedly to check if he hit a person on the road because he mistrusts his experiences.

What Treatment Methods are Used with a Cognitive Approach

Cognitive theories about the origin of OCD appear to fall between psychodynamic and behavioral explanations. This is because these theories focus on cognitions like thoughts or images that are internal to obsessive-compulsives but affect behaviors and patterns of reinforcement. Two main cognitive techniques have been used in OCD treatment.

1. Challenging of obsessional thoughts has been performed using Albert Ellis' Rational Emotive Therapy (RET).[43]

2. Cognitive therapists have challenged negative automatic thoughts using Aaron Beck's Cognitive Therapy, which focuses on negative automatic thoughts rather than on only obsessional thoughts.[44]

Rational Emotive Therapy (RET)

The essential element of this treatment involves determining what types of generalized irrational thoughts and mistaken assumptions control the client's negative feelings of anxiety, discomfort, and tension. The cognitive therapist then works to change the client's irrational thoughts so that he or she no longer feels undue discomfort or anxiety. When the client no longer feels discomfort, theorists believe that compulsions are no longer needed to reduce these negative feelings.

For example, with a compulsive cleaner, a therapist would first help the client realize the irrationality of thoughts like, "If I touch a garbage can, I will become ill and maybe die," or "I must wash my hands many times before I am really clean." The therapist then works with the client to revise the irrational thoughts and develop more accurate perceptions of threat, such as: "Touching garbage cans will not harm me," or "One wash is sufficient to clean my hands." Once the client re-places irrational thoughts with more accurate ones, he or she will no longer perform compulsions because the threat and anxiety that prompted them are no longer present.

RET makes use of Ellis' ABC framework in which **Activating Events** (situational triggers) elicit **Beliefs** (rational and irrational), which are the direct source of emotional and behavioral **Consequences** (obsessions, compulsions, or discomfort).[42, 43] The focus of therapy works to modify these thoughts so that undue feelings of discomfort are no longer experienced. At that point, the compulsive rituals are no longer necessary.

Before therapy begins, the client reads an explanation of RET written in simple terms.[45] Reading this helps the client understand how to analyze irrational beliefs during homework assignments. Treatment begins with the therapist training the client to observe and record cognitions, using pre-coded ABC homework sheets to help discriminate between the actual event and thoughts about the event. During the next therapy stage, the client and therapist rationally dispute the irrational cognitions that the client logged on the homework sheets. The therapist challenges the irrational beliefs using *Socratic questioning,* and the client is instructed to do the same on homework assignments. For example, a client may ask, "What are the chances of that horrible consequence actually occurring? What proof do I have that is really the best explanation?" The therapist requires the client to practice analyzing problems with the pre-coded ABC homework sheets. When homework problems arise, the clinician discusses these with the client, and they analyze the irrational beliefs associated with the problems.

Socratic questioning — *posing a series of questions to force the client to defend irrational beliefs. such as: "What evidence do you have to support that idea? What's the likelihood of such an outcome? What are other possible explanations?"*

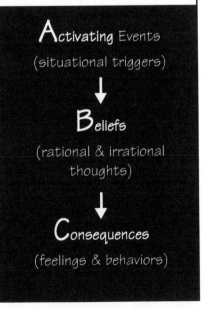

Rational Emotive Therapy (RET) Components

- **Activating Events** — Situational triggers, such as seeing a speed limit sign while driving.

- **Beliefs** — Rational and irrational thoughts, such as "If I am not absolutely sure of the speed limit, I will cause an accident."

- **Consequences** — Obsessions and discomfort; for example, repeatedly going back and checking the speed limit sign.

Activating Events
(situational triggers)

↓

Beliefs
(rational & irrational thoughts)

↓

Consequences
(feelings & behaviors)

Beck's Cognitive Therapy

negative automatic thoughts — *immediate interpretations about the meaning of obsessive thoughts*

Unlike RET, Beck's Cognitive Therapy focuses on challenging negative automatic thoughts or interpretations associated with intrusions. These *negative automatic thoughts* differ from obsessional thoughts in that they are broader, more generalized, and pertain to the meaning clients attach to their obsessive thoughts. For example, a person's automatic thoughts may include: "I'm a dangerous person and may lose control at any moment," "I do not have the skills to cope with my problems," or "People would reject me if they knew about my thoughts." On the other hand, obsessional thoughts might be: "If I do not check the stove again, the house may burn down," or "If I do not wash my hands again, I will catch a disease." These negative interpretations of intrusive experiences are thought to be precursors of obsessional thoughts.[41, 45, 46]

Challenging these automatic thoughts is similar to using RET. The therapist first identifies the themes contained in responses to intrusive experiences, using thought-recording forms that the client completes for homework. The therapist then challenges the client's thinking in a Socratic-like fashion with questions and restatements of the client's reported beliefs. This dialogue forces the client to defend and explain rationally his or her irrational thinking, helping the client realize the unreasonable and detrimental nature of those thoughts. This begins a process of learning new, more adaptive reactions to intrusive, obsessional ideas. Specific cognitive therapy techniques have been developed to address OCD clients' irrational beliefs about the over-importance and need to control thoughts, the probability of danger, and excessive responsibility.[41, 45]

Two of these techniques are Probability Estimation and Responsibility Pie:

- **Probability Estimation.** In Probability Estimation, the therapist and client identify events that would have to occur for the feared disaster to happen and then estimate the actual likelihood of each event. Multiplying these probabilities together usually gives the client a clear idea of exactly how unlikely the feared disaster would be. Often, the probability can be expressed in the number of lifetimes the OCD sufferer would have to live to witness the event.

- **Responsibility Pie.** To estimate responsibility, the therapist draws a pie and asks the client to generate a list of all other persons or organizations that might play some role in the feared outcome (e.g., cooking food that might harm a guest). After assigning percentages of responsibility to each of these (e.g., food maker, storage facilities, transporters, distributors, sellers, etc.), usually very little responsibility is left to the preparer to cause harm.

How Effective are Cognitive Treatments for OCD?

Since obsessive compulsive symptoms are accompanied by and partly maintained by irrational cognitions, one would expect that cognitive therapy would be extremely popular and effective in treating OCD.[47] However, to date, only a few controlled research studies have tested cognitive therapy's effectiveness. Several uncontrolled case studies have shown successful OCD treatment with cognitive therapy alone or in addition to Exposure and Response Prevention.[9, 46] Four published controlled studies of cognitive therapy for OCD have found that it is effective, although not more so than Exposure and Response Prevention alone.[37, 47-49] In addition, the combination of cognitive therapy and Exposure and Response Prevention was no more effective than Exposure and Response Prevention alone.[33, 48]

See pages 60-64 for an explanation of the brain areas and cognitive processes involved in the maintenance and treatment of OCD.

- **RET Effectiveness.** Two controlled studies have been conducted comparing cognitive treatment (based on RET techniques) with Exposure and Response Prevention and found no differences between the two treatments in either study. Both RET and self-controlled Exposure and Response Prevention reduced obsessive-compulsive symptoms as well as social anxiety.[47, 48] Additionally, RET significantly reduced depression scores.[47] Thus, RET may be especially successful for people with OCD who are also depressed.

- **Beck's Cognitive Therapy Effectiveness.** Two controlled studies of Beck's cognitive therapy focused on challenging negative automatic thoughts. Results indicate that this treatment was at least as good as

Since clients with obsessions and mental rituals, but no overt compulsions, have traditionally been very difficult to treat, the successful outcome from cognitive and behavioral treatments combined is quite remarkable.

Exposure and Response Prevention in one trial, with nearly 75 percent of participants improved.[49] Further, an 84 percent success rate was achieved when cognitive therapy was combined with Exposure and Response Prevention in clients who had obsessions and mental rituals but no overt compulsions.[37]

over-valued ideation — *belief that obsessive fears are realistic*

At present, insufficient information exists about whether clients with severe depression, *over-valued ideation*, or obsessions without behavioral rituals benefit more from cognitive therapy than from Exposure and Response Prevention.[44] However, one must still be cautious about the effectiveness of cognitive therapy alone in the treatment of OCD. More research is needed to determine the best cognitive therapy techniques for OCD and which clients will benefit most from this method.

What is the Psychoanalytic Approach to Treating OCD?

Modern psychoanalytic approaches promote the concept that current psychological problems result from historical experiences and personality development. There is no research indicating that this approach is effective in treating OCD. However, psychoanalytic treatment focuses on understanding the disorder and resolving early traumatic experiences that may be related to OCD symptoms. This section reviews:

- Main psychoanalytic theories regarding OCD's origin

- Main principles of psychoanalytic treatment

- Research literature on psychoanalytic treatment efficacy

Psychoanalytic Theories

Psychoanalytic theorists focus on personality development in the context of early environment to explain OCD. Several defense mechanisms are commonly considered, in some combination, to be related to OCD, including:[50]

regression — *the act of going back in one's mind to an earlier period or an earlier way of functioning*

- ***Regression***. Psychoanalytic theorists have suggested that the origin of OCD is linked to psychosexual development, especially the *anal stage*. Part of the anal stage involves pleasures concerning waste retention. Regression to this stage results in a preoccupation with controlling dirt or *anal-retentiveness*. As a result, the individual may develop magical thinking and rituals regarding cleanliness. For example, a person may believe he or she will become contaminated by germs and die after touching a door handle in a public lavatory. In response to this fear, the individual washes his or her hands or cleans excessively to avoid touching germs on a door handle.

- **Reaction Formation**. Symptoms of OCD can also be understood as an opposite response or "reaction formation" to some underlying impulse that brings about inappropriate behavior patterns. For example, if one feels anger or rage, the person may obsess about hurting other people and perform opposite compulsive rituals, such as calling people to make sure they are still alive.

- **Isolation**. The defense mechanism of isolation involves an attempt to separate an impulse, (e.g., to hurt or kill someone) from the original memories and associated emotions. Individuals displaying this mechanism may deny feelings of anger or rage against others who have hurt them.

- **Undoing**. The majority of compulsive rituals are viewed by psychoanalytic theorists as attempts to undo some underlying, unacceptable impulse or thought. For example, an individual with OCD sees a rock lying on the road and may experience a horrible image of that rock causing an accident to another motorist. The OCD sufferer fears he or she may have intended harm to the motorist, and therefore removes the rock so it will not cause an accident, thereby undoing the unacceptable obsessive thought or impulse. Because underlying interpersonal emotional conflicts are not resolved, the undoing actions are only temporarily successful and must be repeated.

anal stage — *the second stage in Freud's theory of psychosexual development concerned with the retention and expulsion of waste*

anal-retentiveness — *individual derives pleasure from cleanliness and order*

reaction formation — *the process through which unacceptable feelings or impulses are controlled by behaving directly opposite of them (e.g.. someone who cleans compulsively to avoid the unconscious feeling of being unacceptable or dirty)*

isolation — *disconnecting impulses and resulting feelings from the original memories associated with them*

undoing — *either mentally replaying or physically performing an act in an attempt to have a more acceptable ending to a previously unacceptable outcome*

displacement — *having or expressing a feeling toward someone or something other than where it belongs*

- **Displacement.** Obsessive-compulsive individuals often attempt to displace feelings on another person or object to lessen their anxiety regarding that person or object. Thus, some individuals with OCD fear certain objects or situations when they are really much more afraid of something else. These people displace their fear onto otherwise neutral objects that then become obsessional cues.

What Treatment Methods are Used with a Psychoanalytic Approach?

In the past, psychoanalytic treatments often lasted many months or even years. In more recent years, changes in health care have led to the development of short-term psychoanalytic treatments for OCD, in which the clinician attempts to help clients face the sources of their anxiety and understand the ineffective compulsions they use to deal with these defense mechanisms. The main components of psychoanalytic treatment are:

insight — *self-awareness or self-understanding of the underlying dynamics of one's actions*

- Providing *insight*

- Tolerating anxiety

- Psychoanalytic formulation of symptoms and defenses

- Corrective emotional experience in the therapy relationship

- Active confrontation

Providing Insight

interpreting — *the clinician reflects to the client hypotheses regarding the connection between unconscious material and current or conscious feelings or behavior*

anal wishes — *desires based on regression to the anal stage, such as excessive need to maintain order and cleanliness*

Short-term, analytic treatment is very active and involves directly producing insight to the client. The clinician achieves this by exposing the client to underlying conflicts through *interpreting* how the client's current statements and actions reflect underlying conflicts and wishes. One area of interpretation is *anal wishes*. For example, the clinician may ask the client to talk about obsessions and then interpret anal wishes by discussing the client's early experiences in psychosexual development. The clinician would help the client discover how he or she may receive some inner pleasure or satisfaction from maintaining order and cleanliness through excessive washing.

Tolerating Anxiety

Because interpretations can produce great anxiety, clients must have the *ego strength* to withstand anxiety-provoking interpretations and insight.[50] Ego-strength characteristics include being motivated to change, possessing above-average psychological sophistication, and having had a meaningful relationship during childhood.

ego strength — *self-confidence, resourcefulness, stability, and ability to cope with problems and stresses in life situations*

Psychoanalytic Formulation of Symptoms and Defenses

After taking the client's personal history and making sure he or she meets selection criteria, (e.g., ego strength) for short-term psychoanalytic treatment, the clinician develops an analytic formulation that offers a resolution to the client's problems. The clinician communicates this formulation to the client, and they reach an agreement on this view of the problem before proceeding. For example, the clinician may come to an agreement with a client on how obsessions and compulsions surrounding contamination and excessive hand washing relate to early experiences of feeling "dirty" or "unacceptable" during the anal-retentive stage of psychosexual development.[50]

Corrective Emotional Experience in the Therapy Relationship

The early stages of short-term, analytic psychotherapy involve establishing a therapeutic alliance or bond between the clinician and the client. This bond facilitates a *corrective emotional experience* and helps the client solve conflicts. Using the *positive transference* that often occurs as a result of an established therapeutic alliance, the client demonstrates a feeling of security about interactions with the clinician. For example, the client may respond to an older female clinician as if she were the mother with whom he or she had a very positive relationship. The clinician links this type of transference to the client's relationship with his or her parents. The client's recognition of the connection between current feelings for the clinician and past relationships helps establish an atmosphere for a corrective emotional experience.

corrective emotional experience — *when a client re-experiences with the therapist an old, chronic conflicting pattern of behavior, such as extreme dependency, and the therapeutic relationship allows for a different healing outcome to the old pattern of behavior*

positive transference — *the client recalls and relives pleasant experiences, feelings, and memories from the past as if they were occurring in the present*

Positive transference can be a powerful motivating force, compelling the client to give up maladaptive behaviors. For example, clients may come to understand that they developed contamination obsessions and cleaning compulsions to be accepted by their parents. After experiencing unconditional acceptance from the clinician, these clients may learn that parental love does not really depend on remaining clean.[50]

Active Confrontation

The next stage of short-term, analytic psychotherapy involves actively working on the central focus agreed to at treatment beginning. The clinician directly confronts the client with paradoxical behavior patterns and uses clear examples to clarify the connection between current difficulties and past experiences. From time to time, the clinician summarizes what has been learned and points out progress made.

During the course of short-term psychodynamic treatment, the clinician continually encounters the client's defense mechanisms. These defenses may involve:

- Denial of excessive compulsive rituals
- Resistance to discussing obsessions
- Rationalizing the compulsion as logical

Clarifying and resolving the client's defenses throughout treatment helps clients in two ways. First, they gain insight into early events in childhood that produce obsessive-compulsive symptoms. Second, they continue moving toward treatment goals.

The clinician interprets the client's transference, defenses, and current symptoms. Clinicians may point out to clients how disruptive obsessions and compulsions have become because they refuse to face their degree of social and occupational impairment. For example, a clinician may interpret a client's harming obsessions and checking rituals as an undoing of an impulse to harm or kill another person. Psychoanalytic theorists believe that once these thoughts and feelings become conscious, the client will resolve previous conflicts and no longer exhibit OCD symptoms.[50]

How Effective is Psychoanalytic Treatment of OCD?

Unfortunately, there are no adequate outcome research studies on psychodynamic treatments for OCD. In fact, one appraisal of psychodynamic therapy for OCD concluded that cure of even uncomplicated cases by this approach is uncommon.[29] Although research fails to confirm psychodynamic treatments as effective for OCD, this approach may help some clients work out early traumatic experiences that may be troubling to them in other spheres (e.g., social anxiety in the presence of others). Freed of OCD's debilitating symptoms, clients may be able to work on coexisting psychological issues of denial, avoidance, and dependency that may have been involved in the development and persistence of OCD.[51]

What is the Group Therapy Approach to Treating OCD?

In this era of managed care and health care reform, using group behavior psychotherapy to treat OCD can be cost-effective as well as therapeutically useful. First, group therapy is more cost-effective than individual OCD therapy because it requires far fewer staff hours to treat the same number of clients. Second, group OCD treatment increases the availability of therapy for areas with limited, trained behavior therapists.[52] Third, therapeutic factors uniquely associated with group therapy may enhance the treatment efficacy of individual behavior therapy. These therapeutic factors include:

Individuals who complete group therapy may feel more comfortable joining community OCD support groups because the stigma and shame of the disorder has been removed.[53]

- **Universality**. The awareness that other clients suffer similar symptoms and the growing understanding that OCD is widespread, help to break down the client's feelings of loneliness and isolation. This is especially helpful because OCD sufferers often isolate themselves due to the embarrassing nature of their symptoms. Sharing feelings and symptoms with others having similar problems helps to overcome the stigma, shame, and loneliness associated with the illness.[52]

- **Altruism**. In a group, clients with OCD come to realize that they have something to contribute to others in terms of suggestions, support, feedback, and reassurance.[52] By helping others, they begin to regain a sense of self worth.

- **Vicarious Learning**. Members of an OCD treatment group can learn by observing others working through similar issues. Because clients listen to others engage in goal setting and behavioral treatments, group members teach and learn from each other as well as acting as motivating examples.

- **Interpersonal Learning**. Clients with OCD often lose perspective as to what is normal behavior. Most group members suffer from different OCD symptoms. Therefore, several members in any group will behave quite normally in many areas of their lives that are problematic for other group members. Group members can learn from each other appropriate behavior for the "normal" person and set goals accordingly.[52]

- **Role Flexibility**. Each member can act both as a client and as a facilitator. Role flexibility enables group members to work as facilitators, coaches, and guides for one another.[52]

- *Group Cohesiveness*. Cohesive groups have a sense of trust, warmth, understanding, acceptance, and solidarity. Setting goals in the presence of the group is an important motivating factor because members are aware that they must share their progress with others at the next meeting. The group atmosphere often helps clients develop larger social support networks as well as spend less time ruminating.[53]

group cohesiveness — the degree to which group members work together for the benefit of each other and the group as a whole

What Treatment Methods are Used with Group Therapy?

There are well-developed guidelines describing the logistics and screening procedures used to manage OCD groups.[53-56] Treatment methods discussed in this section focus on two similar yet distinct behavioral group therapy programs:

1. Methods used in a psychoeducational and support group for OCD clients. These can help clients who are also receiving or have received individual behavior therapy or medication therapy.

2. Methods used in group behavioral treatment that includes In-vivo and Imagined Exposure as well as Response Prevention.

Psychoeducational Group Therapy

Psychoeducational support groups help clarify the nature of OCD and available treatments. They are intended to facilitate concurrent treatment or to help clients and their families decide on what treatment they would like.

A typical psychoeducational and support group may meet once a week for 10 weeks to educate clients and families about OCD and to provide a support network.[54, 55] The outline can follow that of a self-help book for OCD sufferers, such as <u>When Once Is Not Enough</u>, <u>Getting Control</u>, or <u>Stop Obsessing</u>.[57-59] Each session includes an informal lecture topic covered in the session's first 45 minutes. The final 30 to 45 minutes of the session is left open for questions and discussion of the topic covered.

The following lists each session's objectives:

- **Session 1**. Facilitator presents the group's purpose and goals as well as an overview of OCD symptoms and prevalence data.

- **Session 2.** Facilitator reviews OCD diagnostic criteria with relevant examples similar to symptoms found among group members as well as information about the relationship between OCD and other mental disorders.

- **Session 3.** Facilitator leads a discussion of what causes OCD and why it persists, often enhanced by a discussion of OCD-associated cognitions (e.g., irrational beliefs and inaccurate risk assessment).

- **Session 4**. Group members receive instruction on OCD's biological basis, including information on the serotonin hypothesis and brain structures linked to OCD, followed

Chapter 4 reviews the biological basis for OCD and medication treatments.

Subjective Units of Distress scale (SUDs) — *a scale ranging from 10-100 with 10 being the least anxiety provoking and 100 being the most anxiety provoking. The SUDs scoring system allows the client to express exactly how upsetting or distressing certain stimuli are in comparison to other anxiety experiences. For more information, refer to page 13 in chapter 2*

Chapter 4 reviews medication options for treating OCD.

possibly by a review of the research on the efficacy of antidepressant medication treatment.

- **Session 5.** Facilitator gives an overview of OCD behavior therapy, covering Exposure and Response Prevention. The group leader teaches clients to rate and rank their obsessions and compulsions on the *Subjective Units of Distress scale (SUDs)*. Each client identifies approximately 10 situations, events, or objects that cause anxiety and ranks each according to how much anxiety it provokes. The facilitator may demonstrate gradual In-vivo Exposure, using this to illustrate the effectiveness of individual OCD behavior therapy.

- **Session 6.** Participants receive information about Exposure and Response Prevention and encouragement for group members to try relatively simple Exposure and Response Prevention tasks during the session. For instance, an individual who fears being contaminated by touching another person may be asked to shake hands with one of the leaders or another group member without washing immediately afterward.

- **Session 7.** The group discusses the family's role in accommodating OCD and helping during treatment. Because family members can both help and hinder behavioral treatment's effectiveness, the group leader spends time explaining how the family members should and should not behave around the client, especially during behavioral treatment.

- **Session 8.** Facilitator discusses current medications available for treating OCD, focusing on clomipramine, fluoxetine paroxetine, fluvoxamine, and sertraline as well as the side effects and limitations of pharmaco-therapy, (e.g., augmenting agents occasionally used to treat OCD, such as lithium, buspirone, and clonazepam).

- **Session 9.** Facilitator discusses factors that promote successful treatment, such as active involvement of the client and family regardless of the treatment form used. At the end of the session, the group leaders discuss relapse prevention and the fact that OCD is a chronic disorder that may never completely subside.

- **Session 10.** The facilitator summarizes the previous sessions, discusses future directions for OCD research, and reviews group members' plans and involvement in current therapies.

Behavioral Treatment Group Therapy

Applying Exposure and Response Prevention in a group setting requires identifying clients most likely to successfully respond in such a setting. Clinicians should follow these five steps before starting the group.[53, 56]

1. **Conduct a Diagnostic Assessment.** This involves making sure of an accurate diagnosis of OCD and possible coexisting conditions. Clients with schizophrenia and severe depression may manifest OCD-like symptoms, yet they would not respond well to group behavior therapy.

2. **Assess Symptom Type and Severity.** By quantifying the degree of subjective distress caused by OCD symptoms, clinician and client measure improvement during and after treatment. Individuals with a score above 30 on the Yale-Brown Obsessive-Compulsive Scale (see appendix A for a review of the Y-BOCS), are often not good group candidates because their daily functioning is too severely disabled. Individual treatment or pharmacotherapy may better serve these clients until their symptoms are more manageable.

3. **Recommend Psychoeducational Group Therapy Sessions**. Discussion of group composition and process helps clients make a smooth transition into the intensive and interactive behavioral treatment group sessions that will follow.

4. **Discuss Treatment Options.** The group leader and client should discuss treatment options, getting a firm understanding of Exposure and Response Prevention, without which the client may be too frightened to enter such a treatment program. In such cases, the clinician discusses with the client other treatment options including individual therapy or pharmacotherapy. Fearful clients may choose to join a group after engaging in other therapy.

5. **Develop a Hierarchy of Anxiety-evoking Stimuli.** This is the final step before intensive, group behavioral treatment begins. A treatment staff member completes this task individually with each client. The therapist and client use the Subjective Units of Distress (SUDs) Scale (see page 13 in chapter 2 for a description of SUDs scales), to create a list of approximately 25 items or situations that cause anxiety to differing degrees. The clinician and client order the items from least threatening to most threatening based on the scores assigned to each situation. This hierarchy is then ready for use during the group treatment.

There are two major phases of group behaviour treatment: the intensive treatment phase and the maintenance treatment phase.

- **Intensive Treatment Phase.** The group leader conducts two-hour sessions once or twice weekly over a period of up to 12 weeks with groups of 6 to 10 clients. During these sessions, each client is exposed to at least one situation listed on his or her hierarchy and is prevented from engaging in rituals. For example, an individual who fears being contaminated by a garbage can would be asked to touch a garbage can and then refrain from washing or cleaning rituals. An individual who fears the number 13 may be asked to take 13 steps and then refrain from undoing this.

  For those obsessions impossible to introduce using In-vivo Exposure during the group session, the client is asked to imagine that situation as vividly as possible. For example, a compulsive checker would be asked to imagine leaving the house without checking any of the door locks, stove, or oven. To achieve this with the best possible results, the clinician and client construct a detailed script during an individual session that will be imagined during the group therapy session. To accommodate other group members' needs, scripts are generalized across different members' obsessive fears, while each client pictures his or her own specific scenario.

  In the last 30 minutes of the group session, the clinician focuses on assigning each client homework tasks similar to the Exposure and Response Prevention tasks described above. An individual who fears hitting people with a car would be assigned to drive around until those obsessions arose and then refrain from turning the car around and checking the road for injured pedestrians. The client, clinician, and other group members take part in assigning Exposure and Response Prevention tasks.

The first 30 minutes of each subsequent session generally consist of discussing the clients' experiences with the homework tasks. Those clients who were successful in their homework assignments are assigned the next situation or scene from their hierarchy until the most feared item in each client's hierarchy is introduced.

In the final sessions, the therapist presents the client with several situations simultaneously. This may be done In-vivo or in imagination. An example of a multiple In-vivo Exposure and Response Prevention task may include a client being asked to shake a person's hand, touch a trash can, pick up something from the bathroom floor, and touch the lavatory door handle, all without cleaning. A multiple, Imagined Exposure and Response Prevention task may include asking an individual to imagine:

- Not checking the car at night to make sure it hasn't been stolen
- Parking the car without checking the door locks, parking brake, and trunk
- Leaving the house without checking to make sure the iron, oven, stove, and curling iron are off

Once again, the specific tasks that individuals perform or imagine depend on their particular obsessions and compulsions. The exposure tasks for group treatment are very similar to those presented during individual Exposure and Response Prevention.

- **Maintenance Treatment Phase.** After the intensive therapy phase, clients often meet in behavior group therapy sessions spaced out gradually over the next few months.[53-56] These extra sessions motivate and support clients as they continue with exposure activities on their own. Group leaders also encourage clients to join local OCD support groups, if available.

What are the Limitations of Group Therapy for OCD?

Group behavioral therapy for OCD has some potential limitations, including:

- **Difficulty Organizing a Treatment Group.** In some settings, the small number of OCD sufferers who seek treatment may prevent the formation of a group of adequate size. At least six clients are needed to begin a group.[52]

- **Fearing that New Symptoms will be Acquired.** Although some clients fear acquiring new OCD symptoms, studies on behavioral group therapy for OCD show this very rarely happens.[52] If it does occur, the group leader can refer the client to individual therapy.

- **Noncompliance with Treatment.** This may occur because of a problem with a homework task. A discussion of the task and problem solving usually results in a more appropriate homework assignment with which the client will comply.

- **Missed Therapy Sessions.** Clients may avoid coming to the group if they failed to do homework tasks. To resolve the problem, the group leader can contact these clients and rework the homework tasks at a more appropriate difficulty level.

How Effective is Group Therapy for OCD?

As yet, there is no research studying the effectiveness of combining individual and group therapy for OCD treatment.

Group therapy is becoming a more common form of OCD treatment either as a replacement to individual behavior therapy or as an adjunct treatment to individual therapy. Unfortunately, limited information exists on the effectiveness of educational and support groups for OCD. Early uncontrolled studies of OCD behavioral group therapy indicate that group Exposure and Response Prevention techniques effectively reduce OCD symptom severity in about 75 percent of participants.[56, 60, 61] A controlled study that utilized detailed screening criteria for group inclusion and specific, step-by-step procedures found that behavioral group therapy was just as effective as individual behavior therapy at treatment completion as well as at a six-month follow-up.[53, 62] The only difference between the two treatments was that individual behavior therapy improved symptoms more quickly than group behavioral treatment.[62]

What is the Family Therapy Approach to Treating OCD?

Clinicians often recommend marital and family therapy as an adjunctive treatment for OCD, especially when the client indicates that there are significant communication problems or conflicts at home. When the client is married or lives with family, this therapy can be helpful in facilitating treatment gains as well as preventing relapse. Spouses and family members benefit greatly from being involved with the treatment and learning more about the disorder and how to cope with it. They begin to understand that it is not their fault that a family member suffers from OCD. They also learn effective means of coping instead of reinforcing or exacerbating the symptoms. Most importantly, learning about OCD lessens the stigma and shame associated with "mental disorders," which helps families to function more responsibly.[6,18]

The family's role in successful OCD treatment is twofold:

1. **They should be supportive towards the individual with OCD rather than angry or impatient.** Hostile family reactions are especially discouraging to OCD sufferers and may lead to treatment dropout or failure.[63] However, family members should clearly express their concerns about OCD symptoms and encourage or even insist that their relative seek treatment.

2. **Family members should refrain from overly accommodating and reinforcing the individual's obsessions or compulsions.** Family members often reinforce the disorder unknowingly because they hate to see a loved one suffer through exhausting, compulsive rituals. In trying to help, family members may facilitate OCD symptoms and even perform the compulsions with and for the client.[18] Although these behaviors may temporarily help reduce the client's anxiety, they can exacerbate the disorder and its symptoms by reinforcing the obsessions and compulsions as rational and necessary. Although difficult to stand by and watch, family members should be discouraged from assisting in the client's avoidance behaviors and compulsive rituals.

Family accommodation to their relative's OCD symptoms should be deliberately reduced during behavioral treatment.

What Treatment Methods are Used with Family Therapy

Family members may be helpful assistants during the behavior therapy process. The most helpful family members will be adults (including spouses, partners, parents, or other relatives), whom the client considers to be supportive and not overly intrusive in the client's life. Several components of family treatment are often employed.[18, 56] These include:

- **Family Education**. Family members who will be assisting during treatment should attend some early sessions of the client's therapy to learn more about the symptoms of OCD, its etiology, and treatment methods. Educational sessions could be held individually with the client or in a group setting with other OCD families.

- **Support Training during Exposure and Response Prevention**. Family assistants will need to learn to be helpful when the client practices Exposure and Response Prevention homework. The clinician can recommend what to say and do during Exposure homework. For example, the therapist may recommend that the relative no longer reassure the client. Instead, the family member may say, "I'm sorry, but Dr. _____ told me not to reassure you about your fears of hurting other people."

- **Reducing Family Accommodation**. In addition to supporting clients when they expose themselves to feared situations, family members will need to reduce their accommodation to the client's OCD symptoms. This usually means not doing tasks for the client and not performing rituals or checking at the client's request. For example, the clinician may advise a family member not to take out the trash, wash hands, or check the stove, even if the client requests it. These changes should be agreed upon together by the client, the clinician, and the family member.

- **Communication and Problem-solving Training**. In some families, the client and a family member have learned to communicate in angry ways or fail to discuss family problems related to OCD. When this happens, the clinician may ask the client and family member to discuss OCD-related problems during the session. In this way, the clinician can stop ineffective, angry interchanges and encourage clear communication and problem solving. For example, the clinician might stop the relative from yelling at the client about using the bathroom too much and ask what he or she would like to ask the client to do instead. The clinician could then help negotiate a solution, such as reducing time in the bathroom, as part of the client's Exposure and Response Prevention homework.

How Effective is Family Therapy for OCD?

At the present time, very few studies have investigated the benefits of family therapy. Several case reports have indicated that involving spouses or parents in behavioral treatment is very useful.[18] Surprisingly, two controlled studies have shown that including spouses as assistants during Exposure and Response Prevention did not improve the clients' outcomes any more than uninvolved spouses. However, in a different study of family members in India, clients who were assisted by various types of relatives had more benefit than clients who were not helped by relatives.[18]

Researchers have also studied multiple family treatment. When several family members participated together as a group with clients in behavioral treatment, clients showed considerable improvement in OCD symptoms.[56] Thus, it seems that including relatives in the behavioral treatment process can be very helpful.

Behavioral treatments are very successful in helping people with OCD. Using these treatments in a group setting or including family members may enhance the overall treatment program for some clients. However, many people (25 percent or more) are uncomfortable participating in behavior therapy and find relief from their symptoms through the use of medications. Other clients may respond well to the use of medications in combination with behavior therapy. The next chapter reviews how medications work in reducing OCD symptoms, commonly prescribed medications, and the research comparing the effectiveness of medication treatment versus behavioral treatment for OCD.

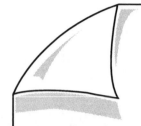

Therapy Notes
From the Desk
of Pat Owen

Saw Amy and Jim P. together. SRI medication is helping mood, and she seemed to have more energy. Jim is frustrated, but still supportive. He agreed to help her with homework assignments without accommodating her OCD too much. Plan seems workable.

She listed her triggers for OCD symptoms and will begin exposure this week. Plan: she'll do exposure and stop repetitions to first four items on her hierarchy list— husband will review her progress Sunday and Wednesday. Scheduled next three appointments. She'll call if problems arise between appointments.

Chapter Four: Medical Treatments for Obsessive Compulsive Disorder

---

Diary of Amy P.

July 1

Have seen Owen three times now. Jim's been great, thank God for his help. The pills seem to help relieve the worry some, and I'm more in control. I need to ask Owen about my sleep problems. I wonder if these are because of the medication? i'm starting to feel better — finally! I didn't have to repeat walking steps at all today. I still have bad times, especially when the baby is cranky and I'm tired. But, I finally feel like I am going to lick this!

This chapter answers the following:

- **What is the Role of Genetics in the Origin of OCD?** — *This section reviews evidence for genetic underpinnings of OCD.*

- **How are Brain Structures and Chemicals Related to OCD?** — *This section reviews relevant research on neuro-anatomy and biochemical functioning in the brain.*

- **What Medications are Used to Treat OCD?** — *This section reviews medications used in OCD treatment, common side effects, and treatment recommendations for co-existing mental disorders. In addition, this section reviews the efficacy research for medication treatment.*

- **What Other Medical Treatments are Available for OCD?** — *This section reviews less-common treatments for OCD.*

- **How Effective are Medications versus Behavior Therapy in Treating OCD?** — *This section reviews research comparing the two treatment approaches.*

Until recently, psychological factors such as childhood trauma, disordered personality, and primitive coping skills have been identified as critical in the development of OCD. However, recent research results have prompted a dramatic shift in our understanding of the causes of OCD. Biological, rather than psychological, factors are now considered most important in the development of OCD. This chapter reviews the evidence for this biological emphasis including:

- Role of genetics in the origin of OCD

- Brain structure and brain chemical abnormalities

- Medications used to treat OCD and their mechanism of action

- Other, less-common medical treatments, such as neurosurgery

- Research comparing medication treatment to behavior therapy

What is the Role of Genetics in the Origin of OCD?

OCD often afflicts more than one member of the same family. However, it is unlikely that this is a consequence of environmental elements such as "learned behavior"; because symptom presentation often differs greatly between individual family members. Research results demonstrate that genetic, rather than environmental, factors more likely account for the tendency of OCD to occur in families. This evidence indicates that:

- OCD and obsessive-compulsive behavior occur more frequently in parents and children of OCD sufferers.[64-66]

- Approximately 40 percent of OCD sufferers have a relative also afflicted with OCD.[67]

- The likelihood that twins will both have OCD is higher for *monozygotic* than for *fraternal* twins.[65, 67]

- Family and twin studies suggest that one or a few *genes* are more likely than multiple genes to be critical in OCD development.[67]

Further evidence for a genetic cause of OCD results from family studies suggesting that OCD is related to other anxiety conditions and depressive disorders. These studies indicate that OCD, anxiety disorders, and depression may share a similar underlying basis. The prominent and excessive worries as well as the frequent avoidance behaviors commonly exhibited in OCD support its current classification as an anxiety disorder. Depression and co-existing anxiety conditions commonly complicate OCD. Research studies reveal that in OCD sufferers:

- Two-thirds develop depression during their lifetime.[68-71]

- Ten percent also have bipolar (manic-depressive) illness.[69, 70, 72]

monozygotic — *derived from the same fertilized egg and identical genetic make-up*

fraternal — *dizygotic or non-identical twin derived from separate eggs and possessing different genetic characteristics*

gene — *DNA sequence located at a specific site on a chromosome that codes for a certain characteristic(s); the biological basis of heredity*

- Forty percent have an additional anxiety diagnosis, such as: Social Phobia, Panic Disorder, or Generalized Anxiety Disorder.[68-70]

There is also evidence linking OCD and *Tourette's Syndrome*.[73, 74] Tourette's Syndrome (TS) is a neurological condition characterized by intermittent tics. Most people with TS can suppress their tics for short periods of time with considerable effort. The resulting discomfort eventually triggers the re-emergence of the tics. Research supports that OCD and TS have a *genetic link* because:

- Over 50 percent of TS sufferers also have OCD symptoms.[64]

- OCD sufferers are four times more likely to have a family member with tics or TS than individuals without OCD.[65-67, 75]

- Both TS and OCD seem to involve an abnormality in the *basal ganglia*.[76, 77]

How are Brain Structures and Chemicals Related to OCD?

For many years, researchers have found specific abnormalities in some areas of the brain and in some chemicals in the brain related to OCD. Specific areas of the brain and their underlying biochemistry are now considered the most important factors in OCD development. In addition, behavioral effects elicited by certain brain injuries may provide some important clues about specific brain areas most likely to mediate OCD symptoms. Significant clues to OCD's link with specific areas of and chemicals within the brain also come from:

- Studying the biological causes of other illnesses that produce OCD-like symptoms

- Neuroimaging studies that examine structural and functional differences between those with OCD and others

- The neuroanatomy of the brain

- Biochemical factors

The most common anxiety conditions reported to co-exist with OCD are Panic Disorder (10-35 percent), Social Phobia (10-40 percent), and Generalized Anxiety Disorder (5-40 percent).[68-70]

Tourette's Syndrome — *involuntary, sudden, rapid, recurrent, motor movements or vocalizations*

genetic link — *tendency for genes that code for separate characteristics to be inherited together even though found at different locations on the chromosomes*

basal ganglia — *brain area containing several structures, including the caudate nucleus, putamen, and substantia nigra, the primary function of which is to initiate and control body movement*

Researchers suggest that vulnerability for TS and OCD may be "coded" by the same or similar genes.[67]

Specific Brain Areas Involved

Two primary areas are most often implicated in the development of OCD — the basal ganglia and the pre-frontal and orbito-frontal brain regions.

Basal Ganglia

Evidence implicating the relationship of the basal ganglia with OCD centers on these observations:

thalamus — *brain area with multiple connections to other brain regions. It primarily functions as a relay station for body sensations, including pain and temperature*

- Abnormal behaviors (e.g., rituals) likely involve the basal ganglia because that area's primary function is to control initiation and modulation of movement.[10-12, 78-81] Additional functions include processing and filtering of information that is fed back (via the *thalamus*) to help control behavior and thinking.

neurotransmitters — *chemical messengers that transmit signals from one nerve cell to another to elicit physiological responses*

- This is the site of a particularly rich array of *neurotransmitters* and multiple *receptors*.

Research findings that support the importance of the basal ganglia in OCD include:

receptors — *membrane-bound protein molecules with a highly specific shape that facilitate binding by neurotransmitters or drugs*

- In animals, damage to the basal ganglia is linked to the repeated performance of behaviors that resemble compulsive rituals.[15, 16, 81-84]

- Patients afflicted with Parkinson's Disease or Huntington's Chorea, diseases that arise from deterioration of nerve cells within the basal ganglia, have an increased risk of subsequently developing OCD symptoms.[11, 85]

Pre-frontal and Orbito-frontal Brain Regions

The circuit and linking of the multiple brain areas involved in OCD all perform overlapping functions.

Evidence implicating frontal lobe involvement in OCD relies on frontal-lobe identified functions and results from neuroimaging studies (reviewed on pages 61-62).

The frontal lobes of the brain include a pre-frontal and an orbito-frontal area, where main functions include:[10-12, 78-81]

- Filtering, prioritizing, and organizing information received by the brain

- Suppressing or delaying responses to extraneous or unimportant stimuli

- Engaging in logical, prioritized, consequence-based, decision making functions

- Regulating and "fine-tuning" movements and complex behaviors activated by the basal ganglia

These functions are critical to spontaneity and the expression of emotion. Since these attributes are often considered impaired in people with OCD, the frontal lobes likely have an important role in OCD symptom expression.

Other Illnesses that Produce OCD-like Symptoms

Other illnesses or conditions that damage the basal ganglia and its connections to the brain's frontal lobes can elicit OCD-like symptoms (e.g., encephalitis, anoxia, and carbon-monoxide poisoning).

See pages 9 and 16 for more complete lists of medical conditions associated with OCD symptoms.

Recent studies identify a particularly fascinating link between Sydenham's Chorea and OCD that supports the importance of the basal ganglia in the production of OCD symptoms.[13, 86-88] These studies indicate that individuals afflicted with Sydenham's Chorea have an elevated risk of subsequently developing OCD symptoms.[13, 86-88] Sydenham's Chorea is a rare, neurological condition that results from damage to the basal ganglia, triggered by the spread of group A, beta-hemolytic streptococcus bacteria into the brain. *Antibodies* produced by the immune system to combat this invading bacteria damage basal ganglia along with the streptococcus bacteria. This occurs because the antibody misidentifies the basal ganglia nerve cells as bacteria and destroys them. Destruction of the basal ganglia cells produces the abnormal movements of Sydenham's Chorea as well as the development of OCD.

antibodies — *complex protein molecules created specifically to destroy organisms deemed to be dangerous*

Neuroimaging Studies in OCD

Brain imaging studies use x-rays, *CAT scans*, and *MRI* examinations to evaluate structural and functional differences in those with and without OCD. Results from structural brain imaging studies conducted in subjects with OCD reveal inconsistent findings regarding the size and shape of the

CAT scans — *Computerized Axial Tomography; computer-assisted x-rays*

MRI — *Magnetic Resonance Imaging*

caudate nucleus — *a basal ganglia component involved in the voluntary control of movement*

caudate nucleus of the basal ganglia , a primary area of the brain implicated in OCD. Additionally, research suggests that people with OCD may have abnormal proportions of one brain area to another. These findings are not particularly impressive nor consistent. However, they do support the premise that brain abnormalities exist in those with OCD.[10, 76, 78, 89-91]

PET — *Positron Emission Tomography*

SPECT — *Single Photon Emission Computerized Tomography*

There is even more compelling evidence of brain abnormalities from studies of brain functioning, utilizing *PET*, *SPECT*, and MRI scans. Results using these instruments are not diagnostic (i.e., they can neither "make" nor "break" a specific diagnosis). However, these initial investigations reveal that certain areas of the brain in OCD have abnormal levels of brain activity. Specifically:

- Most OCD subjects have increased brain activity in the orbital-frontal region of the cerebral cortex compared to healthy volunteer subjects.[10, 76, 89, 90]

- Some OCD subjects have increased brain activity in the caudate nucleus within the basal ganglia of the brain compared to healthy volunteer subjects.[10, 76, 89-90]

- Inducing symptoms by exposing those with OCD to their most-feared stimuli during PET or SPECT scans results in increased activation of the orbital-frontal cortex and the basal ganglia.[10, 12, 90]

- Hyperactivity present in the frontal lobe or basal ganglia will resolve after successful treatment with either SRI anti-depressant medication or behavioral therapy.[22]

state like — *a current, non-permanent condition*

trait like — *an enduring condition*

These are particularly exciting results with important and wide-ranging implications. These results suggest that certain brain abnormalities (excess activity in the frontal lobes and basal ganglia) are visible and measurable in most subjects with OCD. These brain abnormalities are considered *state like* rather than *trait like*. That is, inducing OCD symptoms elicits activation of the frontal lobes and the basal ganglia in OCD subjects, and successful treatment results in "normalization" of the activity in these regions. Moreover, these changes in brain activity can be detected whether or not improvement results from medication or behavioral interventions. Although behavioral therapy has traditionally been considered a non-biological treatment, successful OCD treatment with behavioral therapy appears to trigger chemical changes within the brain identical to those observed with successful medication treatment.[22]

The Neuroanatomy of OCD

Certain areas of the brain, including the frontal cortex, basal ganglia, and *limbic system,* are thought to be involved in the production of OCD symptoms. Specifically, neuroimaging studies indicate disturbance in the neural pathways that originate in the orbito-frontal cortex and traverse through the sub-cortical areas of the brain to terminate in the basal ganglia.

limbic system – brain region involved in smell, automatic behaviors, and emotions, that surrounds the midbrain and has extensive connections with the thalamus and brain stem

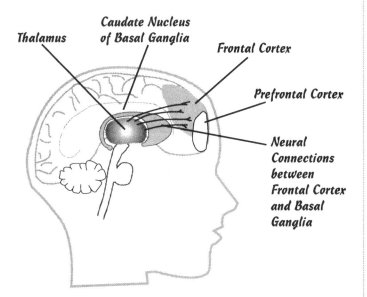

Thalamus

Caudate Nucleus of Basal Ganglia

Frontal Cortex

Prefrontal Cortex

Neural Connections between Frontal Cortex and Basal Ganglia

The circuit from the orbito-frontal to the sub-cortical parts of the brain is critical in the production of OCD symptoms. Information received by the caudate nucleus of the basal ganglia is filtered and then transmitted to the orbito-frontal cortex for further interpretation and potential activation of appropriate responses. When this circuit is functioning properly, the portion originating in the basal ganglia and projecting to the cerebral cortex has an inhibitory effect. That is, increasing activity within the orbito-frontal to basal-ganglia pathway should trigger feedback from the returning portion of the loop. The resulting feedback suppresses further activation, preventing excess or superfluous behaviors.

Some research indicates that input from the emotional (limbic) brain to the cortex areas involved with cognitions is stronger than vice versa. Therefore, the effects of behavior therapy and medication treatments may be due to the strengthening of these weaker connections.

Several authors have postulated that inadequate filtering of anxiety-related inputs by the caudate nucleus could trigger the orbito-frontal cortex to initiate excessive behaviors, such as rituals. Impairment in the feedback mechanism could also encourage excess activation of behaviors or reduced ability to suppress behaviors once they occur. Evidence supporting this model includes:

- Patients with injuries to the orbito-frontal circuit demonstrate an impaired ability to suppress their responses to irrelevant stimuli.[10, 79, 90]

- OCD subjects have abnormal results on tests that assess their ability to suppress inappropriate responses (suppression failure).[16, 79, 90, 92, 93]

- Abnormal activity in the basal ganglia occurs in OCD subjects when they exhibit suppression failure on tests administered during SPECT scans.[10]

Biochemical Factors in OCD

Most theories concerning OCD's potential causes include some type of abnormal function in the neural circuits between the frontal lobe and the basal ganglia within the brain. Serotonin and dopamine are the primary neurotransmitters for the neural circuits that connect these areas.

Serotonin is one of the major neurotransmitters within the brain.[94] Relatively high concentrations of serotonin are present in the *hypothalamus* and the basal ganglia. A variety of physiological functions are modulated by serotonin, including pain perception; aggressive, sexual, and impulsive behaviors; mood, anxiety; and sleep, temperature, appetite, movement, and balance.[94, 95]

hypothalamus — *A small brain structure critically involved in survival functions, such as temperature regulation, heart rate, blood pressure, feeding behavior, water intake, and emotional and sexual behavior*

Although OCD has historically been linked to abnormal serotonin function, "The Serotonin Hypothesis of OCD" is based primarily on the finding that medications effective in treating OCD are limited to antidepressants with potent or selective effects on serotonin neurotransmission.[75, 96-100]

Research results suggest that serotonin function is abnormal in OCD and that successful treatment with SRI (Serotonin Reuptake Inhibitor), medications appears to "correct" this abnormality.[96, 98-103] Interestingly, a relapse can be induced by manipulating the amount of serotonin available during SRI treatment. This suggests that the therapeutic benefits achieved by the SRI medications in OCD depend on serotonin. At the same time, research indicates that the other neurotransmitters (norepinephrine and dopamine) appear to be normal in OCD subjects, further confirming the unique importance of serotonin.[96, 99, 100, 104]

Despite SRI medications remaining the cornerstone of treatment, renewed interest exists in other chemicals in OCD (e.g., neuropeptides and hormones). However, no consistent findings have yet emerged.

However, no specific test concerning serotonin can be used to diagnose OCD. In fact, most people with OCD have normal blood levels of serotonin.[75, 96, 100, 105] Moreover, abnormal serotonin function can also be present in healthy volunteers without psychiatric symptoms as well as in subjects with depression, panic, anorexia, bulimia, or schizophrenia.[95] Since it is widely distributed and involved in so many different functions, the lack of consistent or specific serotonin abnormalities in OCD is not particularly surprising.[94] It is also possible that the abnormal findings involving serotonin in OCD do not really represent the main cause of OCD. Instead, perhaps serotonin is only secondarily involved in OCD. That is, the alterations in serotonin may well result from a genetic defect that increases vulnerability for OCD when serotonin abnormalities are present. So, while <u>present</u> in OCD, these abnormalities may not <u>cause</u> OCD.

Here's how the physiology of serotonin neurotransmission works. *Neurons* (which relay signals from the soma to their terminals where they trigger the release of neurotransmitters) and dendrites (which receive messages from receptors and then transmit them to the soma) communicate by releasing neurotransmitters into the *synaptic cleft*. The *pre-synaptic* neuron is responsible for packaging, releasing, and delivering the neurotransmitter into the synapse, where it can diffuse across to the *post-synaptic* neuron. Neurotransmitters attach to a specific post-synaptic *receptor*. The neurotransmitter forms a temporary binding complex with the receptor, analogous to a "lock-and-key" formation.

neurons — *nerve cells consisting of cell bodies or soma, axons*

synaptic cleft — *gap between neurons*

pre-synaptic — *neuronal area proximal to the synapse*

post-synaptic neuron — *area lying adjacent to the nerve terminal that contains the post-synaptic receptors*

Binding of the messenger to the receptor results in a chemical change that leads to a biological response, such as a behavior, a thought, or a reaction. Once delivery of the message occurs, the receptor releases the neurotransmitter back into the synaptic cleft. Most neurotransmitters are subsequently re-absorbed by a specialized re-uptake site located on the pre-synaptic neuron. The re-uptake mechanism is selective for serotonin, dopamine, or norepinephrine, respectively. Once the neurotransmitter re-enters the pre-synaptic side of the neuron, rapid destruction by enzymes such as monoamine oxidase (MAO) occurs. Enzymes are also present in the synapse to destroy neurotransmitters that are not immediately re-absorbed by the re-uptake pump mechanism. There are multiple points of regulation between the pre-synaptic and post-synaptic neurons. Incoming signals received by the post-synaptic receptor result in activation or inhibition of subsequent neuronal activity.

In this way, constant communication occurs between the pre- and post-synaptic neurons in an attempt to maintain homeostasis. For example, increasing amounts of serotonin within the synapse will trigger several reactions designed to "turn-off" or "reduce" further increases in serotonin.

What Medications are Used to Treat OCD?

Medications effective in OCD are limited to antidepressants that potently or selectively block the serotonin re-uptake pump. Such medications are labeled serotonin re-uptake inhibiting (SRI) antidepressants, and are the first-line medication treatments for OCD.[97, 106, 107] SRI antidepressants include the tricyclic antidepressant (TCA), clomipramine (Anafranil®), and the selective serotonin re-uptake inhibitors (SSRI). SSRI medications currently approved by the U.S. Federal Drug Administration for the treatment of OCD include fluoxetine (Prozac®), sertraline (Zoloft®), paroxetine (Paxil®), and fluvoxamine (Luvox®). There are substantial differences in the side effect and safety profile of clomipramine versus the SSRI antidepressants. The table on pages 68-69 highlights the main differences between the two and reports the drugs mechanism of action, common dosages, side-effects, and special concerns. The most serious side-effects and special concerns are noted in **bold** print.[108]

Special Note Regarding Half-Life and Dosing

The long half-life of fluoxetine has several important implications. Usually the time it takes for a medication to achieve a
steady amount within the blood (steady-state concentration) is
estimated by multiplying the *half-life* of the medication by
five. Therefore, it takes at least four to six weeks before
achieving a steady-state concentration with fluoxetine after
initiating treatment or modifying the fluoxetine dose. This
suggests that changing the dose more often than every four to
six weeks is unwise since the amount of fluoxetine available
within the blood has not yet stabilized. Fluoxetine's long half-
life also suggests that less frequent doses may be possible in
some patients without loss of effectiveness. Therefore,
fluoxetine may be particularly advantageous for patients who
often miss doses or are less likely to comply with strict dose
regimens.[108, 109] Changes in dose for sertraline and paroxetine
should reflect steady-state concentrations achieved within
four to five days. Changes in dose for fluvoxamine should
reflect the ability to stabilize within three to four days.

half-life — *the time
required to eliminate 50
percent of a medication
from the body*

*See pages 68-69 for half-
life indciations of treatment medications*

What are the Differences in Medication Treatment of OCD and Depression?

Important differences exist between OCD medication treatment and medication treatment for depression.[107] While many
medications are effective and FDA-approved for the treatment of depression, most antidepressants are ineffective for
treating OCD because they have different mechanisms of
action and effect neurotransmitters other than serotonin. Only
the five medications reviewed on pages 68-69 are FDA-
approved and effective for OCD. They are all potent blockers
of the serotonin re-uptake pump.[106]

Depressive symptoms usually improve much more rapidly
than OCD symptoms. For example, three to four weeks of
effective antidepressant therapy usually results in robust
improvement in depressive symptoms. In addition, a patient
with an initial or uncomplicated episode of depression can
reasonably expect to experience full symptom remission with
appropriate medication.

Name of Medication	Mechanism of Action	Dosages	Half-Life of Medication
Clomipramine	Clomipramine's benefit in OCD is linked to its effects on the serotonin re-uptake pump, but it also has several other chemical effects, including blocking the body's histamine (antihistamine effects) and acetylcholine (anticholinergic effects) receptors.	150-250 mg./day	Approximately a day (19-37 hrs.), so it can be effectively administered in a once-a-day dosing regimen.

SSRI Medications	Mechanism of Action for ALL SSRI's	Dosages	Half-Life of Medication
fluoxetine (Prozac®)	Pharmacological effects are restricted to the selective blockade of the serotonin re-uptake pump[106, 108, 109]	20-80 mg./day	2-4 days for fluoxetine and 7-10 days for nor-fluoxetine (active metabolite)
sertraline (Zoloft®)		50-200 mg./day.	24 hours
paroxetine (Paxil®)		40-60 mg./day	24 hours
fluvoxamine (Luvox®)		200-300 mg./day	12-24 hours

Side-effects	*Special Concerns*
Side effects attributed to the anticholinergic and antihistamine properties of clomipramine include dry mouth, fatigue, sedation, tremor, dizziness, increased heart rate, constipation, and weight gain.[103, 106, 110]	Doses should not exceed 250 mg./day because of link to an unacceptable seizure risk (1-3%). **A 5-7 day supply of clomipramine represents a potentially fatal overdose if taken at once.** Caution should be taken for patients with pre-existing, serious medical conditions, such as: heart disease, a seizure disorder, or certain types of glaucoma. Seizures, abnormal heart rhythms, and coma can occur when ingesting a dose of clomipramine that is only 4-6 times the usual recommended daily dose.[111] Thus, in spite of clomipramine's unparalleled track record in OCD, it is often relegated to a position behind the SSRIs in initial treatment. Clomipramine withdrawal symptoms include headache, insomnia, increased salivation, flu-like symptoms, and diarrhea.

Side-effects	*Special Concerns for All SSRI's*
All: Sexual dysfunction (decreased libido, delayed orgasm, or anorgasmia), decreased appetite, nausea, fatigue, daytime sedation, nervousness, restlessness, and anxiety **fluoxetine:** nervousness, agitation, anxiety, respiratory complaints, headache, nausea, dry mouth, and tremors **sertraline: diarrhea, tremor, dry mouth,** insomnia, decreased libido, nausea, anorexia, ejaculation failure, increased sweating, and increased weight gain **paroxetine:** sexual dysfunction, frequent urination, weakness, fatigue, dizziness, sweating, nausea, somnolence, headache, and constipation **fluvoxamine:** drowsiness, constipation, anorexia, insomnia, nausea, asthenia, somnolence, abnormal ejaculation, nervousness, and dry mouth	Because SSRI medications do not directly influence specific receptors or block the norepinephrine re-uptake pump mechanism, they have a limited side effect and toxicity profile and are relatively safe in overdose. **Except for fluoxetine**, rapid discontinuation of SSRIs is commonly associated with symptoms of withdrawal, which persist for 1-2 weeks.[108] **Paroxetine** is most frequently implicated in withdrawal symptoms.[112] However, similar symptoms can also occur with fluvoxamine and sertraline. Typical SSRI withdrawal symptoms include dizziness, headache, tingling, "electric-shock" sensations, and flu-like symptoms.[108, 113] A single dose of the medication can be used to rapidly block withdrawal symptoms prior to re-instituting a more gradual tapering of the medication. Allow at least 4-6 weeks before achieving a steady-state concentration with fluoxetine when initiating treatment or modifying the dose. When fluvoxamine doses exceed 150 mg./day, administer in two, divided doses/day.

In contrast, OCD medication treatment is characterized by:[25, 97, 106, 107, 114-116]

- Relatively few effective medications.

- Delayed onset (six to 10 weeks) of therapeutic effects.

- Partial improvement in symptoms is the rule (25 to 40 percent); remission is very rare (less than 10 percent).

How Long are Medications Used for Treatment?

Due to its extensive half-life, fluoxetine can be discontinued without an extensive tapering regimen.[108]

The risk of withdrawal symptoms can be dramatically reduced if the dose is gradually reduced over several months. A reasonable rate of dose reduction is 50-100 mg. per month for clomipramine, fluvoxamine, or sertraline and 20 mg. per month for paroxetine.

Once the clinician determines the most effective medication for an OCD patient, treatment should continue for at least a year.[97, 107] OCD patients generally remain improved as long as they continue taking SRI medications. There is some evidence that the SRI medication dose may be reduced after six to nine months in many OCD patients without substantial loss of effectiveness. In fact, several studies have suggested that a 30 to 70 percent decrease in SRI dose is often possible after nine to twelve months of treatment, without substantial loss of therapeutic effects.[117, 118]

Data from controlled studies suggest that most OCD patients relapse fairly rapidly after discontinuing effective medication.[119, 120] To reduce relapse rates, concurrent use of behavioral therapy may be particularly effective when discontinuing medication. Additionally, many routinely recommend a gradual tapering off, rather than an abrupt discontinuation of SRI medication.

How Effective are Medications in the Treatment of OCD?

Overall, when comparing the various SRI treatments, researchers find they show similar effectiveness in reducing OCD symptoms by about 30 percent.[97, 99, 106, 107, 115] However, there are some important differences reported in specific dose recommendations, including:

- The U.S. study of administering 13 weeks of fluoxetine versus a placebo in OCD revealed that 20, 40, and 60 mg. per day of fluoxetine was more effective than the placebo.[121]

- A large, multi-center study of sertraline confirmed its effectiveness at 50, 100, and 150 mg. per day, in the treatment of acute OCD.[122] Sertraline was also effective in reducing relapse during a one-year, extended-treatment study conducted with OCD patients.[123]

- In a large, multi-center study, paroxetine was effective for the treatment of OCD at doses of 40 and 60 mg./day.[124] Paroxetine was also effective in reducing relapse in OCD patients who continued on the drug in a long-term extension study.[125]

- Fluvoxamine was effective for OCD patients in a large, multi-center study at an average daily dose of 250 mg./day.[126]

Research comparing a client's response to one SRI medication based on his or her response to a different SRI may help facilitate treatment decisions. Unfortunately there is little data concerning this important issue. However, a preliminary study comparing 81 OCD patients, who received separate trials of clomipramine and fluoxetine, found:[69, 107]

- Patients who improved with clomipramine were likely (65 percent chance) to also improve during later treatment with fluoxetine.

- Relatively few (20 percent) patients who failed to respond to clomipramine improved during subsequent fluoxetine therapy.

- Patients who improved during fluoxetine therapy were very likely (80 percent) to also improve during clomipramine treatment.

Overall, research on the effectiveness of SRI treatment of OCD indicates that:

- Clomipramine and the SSRIs are effective for OCD.

- SSRI medications have fewer side effects and are safer in overdose than clomipramine.

- Failure to respond to one SRI does not preclude response to another SRI in OCD.

It remains controversial whether clomipramine is more effective than the SSRIs for OCD, but most investigators recommend that a trial of clomipramine is necessary before "giving up" on medication for OCD. That is, clomipramine should always be considered a first-line treatment along with the SSRIs in the treatment of OCD.

SRI Medication can be ineffective for as many as 20 to 25 percent of treated clients.[30, 97, 107] However, certain factors can contribute to the incorrect labeling of an OCD patient as "medication-refractory" or "SRI resistant," including:[30, 97, 107, 114-116]

- Using other medications instead of clomipramine or an SSRI [lack of SRI trial(s)]

- Giving up too soon on a medication (less than six to 10 weeks)

- Taking too low of a medication dose

- Misdiagnosing the disorder as OCD

- Abusing alcohol or drugs

- Not taking the medication as prescribed or routinely missing doses

- Having unreasonable expectations (e.g., expecting symptoms to rapidly improve or disappear)

Education and information about OCD and potential treatment options represents one of the most important components in implementing successful treatment plans. Each of these factors should be considered, explored, and excluded when a patient with OCD fails to benefit from medication treatment. In patients who have depression (without OCD), and show only partial improvement on antidepressant medication, *augmenting* with medication such as lithium, thyroid hormone, or buspirone often results in further improvement. Since medication response is usually partial, augmentation strategies (combined SRI & augmentation agent), are also often attempted in OCD. However, augmenting usually provides no additional benefit for OCD symptoms.

augmenting – *adding in another medication to enhance therapeutic benefits*

The few circumstances where augmentation strategies may prove helpful in OCD include:

- **Co-existing depression.** For OCD patients who also have depression, augmentation with lithium may be helpful in improving the depressive symptoms.[97, 107]

- **Co-existing tic disorders.** For OCD clients with Tourette's Syndrome or a tic disorder, adding in a low dose of neuroleptic medication (e.g., haloperidol or pimozide) often results in both OCD symptoms and the tics improving.[127] Moreover, preliminary reports with the atypical neuroleptic Risperidone[®], added to an SRI medication suggest that further improvement in OCD symptoms may occur even in the absence of a co-existing tic disorder.[75, 128-130]

- **Persistent anxiety.** Adding in clonazepam or buspirone may help to reduce anxiety in OCD when it does not improve with SRI medication alone.

In summary, research findings indicate that augmentation strategies are rarely effective for most people with OCD.

What Alternatives to SRIs are Used in Treating OCD?

Before being considered as "resistant" to SRI medications, a patient should receive separate and adequate trials (lasting more than 10 weeks for each SRI) of at least three of the four SSRI medications (fluoxetine, fluvoxamine, sertraline, paroxetine) and a separate clomipramine trial. Researchers estimate that as many as 20 to 25 percent of those with OCD fail to respond to SRI medication.[30, 97, 107, 114-116] As previously discussed, only a few patients will experience substantial success with augmentation strategies.

Other agents have also been used in the treatment of OCD, including:

- **MAOI antidepressants.** OCD patients who also have severe panic attacks, social phobia, or prominent obsessions about illness, especially bowel complaints (e.g., constipation), may represent a sub-group that is likely to respond to MAOI treatment.[107, 115, 131, 132] It is important to be very cautious, however, when considering MAOI treatment since numerous and potentially fatal food and drug interactions have been identified.[133]

MAOI antidepressants, Phenelzine (Nardil[R]), or tranylcypromine (Parnate[R]), do not appear to be effective for most people with OCD.[97]

- **Cyclic Antidepressant.** Despite encouraging case reports, trazodone (Desyrel[R]) was no more effective than a placebo in treating OCD.[134, 135]

- **Newer Generation, Non-SSRI Antidepressants.** Venlafaxine (Effexor[R]), has been successfully used for OCD in a small study, although a controlled study failed to demonstrate its effectiveness for OCD treatment over a placebo.[136, 137] Nefazodone (Serzone[R]), also yielded mixed results for OCD in initial reports.[138]

- **Anti-anxiety Agents.** Buspirone (BuSpar[R]), clonazepam (Klonopin[R]), and oxazepam (Serax[R]) were initially considered promising for treating OCD.[139-141] However, subsequent studies largely failed to support this effectiveness, although clonazepam has shown some promise as an augmentation strategy in OCD, especially for persistent anxiety.[142, 143]

- **Combined SRI Regimens.** Recently, combined clomipramine/SSRI or SSRI/SSRI regimens have been the focus of considerable interest. Despite widespread clinical use, however, surprisingly little research exists.[144, 145] Researchers speculate that this combined strategy may offer certain advantages, such as enhanced effectiveness or a means of balancing side effects (e.g., using low-dose clomipramine or paroxetine to counter agitation or insomnia elicited by fluoxetine or sertraline). However, this combination can be risky because when the SSRI antidepressants are combined with clomipramine, they substantially elevate clomipramine's plasma concentrations and keep more clomipramine in the active metabolized form. The increased clomipramine blood level can dangerously elevate the risk of toxic reactions and increase side effects. Careful monitoring of clomipramine blood levels is generally recommended to reduce this risk. While promising, further studies are clearly needed to establish the potential efficacy and safety of combining SRI medications in the treatment of OCD.

What Other Medical Treatments are Available for OCD?

Other treatments have also been tried as therapies to reduce OCD. They include neurosurgery and Electroconvulsive Therapy (ECT).

Neurosurgery

Neurosurgery should only be considered an option for OCD patients with severe, incapacitating symptoms who fail to respond to multiple and adequate treatment trials that include SRI medication and behavioral therapy.[115, 146-148] Clinicians typically do not consider neurosurgery unless a patient with OCD fails to respond or tolerate:

- At least three separate and adequate SSRI trials
- An adequate trial of clomipramine
- An adequate trial of behavioral therapy (Exposure and Response Prevention)
- An MAOI trial (phenelzine or tranylcypromine)
- Two or more augmentation strategies (e.g., clonazepam, Risperidone[R])
- An atypical antidepressant trial (i.e., venlafaxine, nefazodone, mirtazapine)
- A combined SSRI and clomipramine trial

In neurosurgery, surgeons create microscopic lesions in the specific brain areas implicated as functionally abnormal in OCD. These lesions are localized to the sites that contain the neural pathways connecting the frontal cortex to the limbic and basal ganglia structures within the brain and are thought to partly correct an abnormally overactive circuit. Several different surgical procedures exist, but *cingulotomy* and *capsulotomy* are the two, most common neurosurgical techniques utilized in OCD. Long-term, follow-up studies of OCD patients who receive neurosurgery reveal that:

- Two and one-half years after cingulotomy, 28 percent (5/18) of previously refractory OCD patients were responders, and 17 percent (3/18) were partial responders.[146]

cingulotomy — removal of the mid-line fold in the outer layer of both sides of the brain, which contain neural pathways from the cortex to the inner brain

capsulotomy — removal of the front part of the internal capsule of the brain, which contains nerves that connect the cerebral cortex to the basal ganglia

- In 26 OCD patients followed for a mean of 10 years after a cingulotomy, 38 percent had substantial improvement, whereas the remainder were considered unchanged (46 percent) or worse (15 percent) after the procedure.[147]

- After capsulotomy, 48 percent (9/19) of OCD patients were rated as improved. Lesions created within the right internal capsule appeared to be associated with the most favorable outcome.[148]

- Serious complications, such as seizures (five percent) or infection (one percent), are rare after neurosurgery for OCD.[115, 146-148]

- No difference in personality or intellectual and memory functions is detectable after neurosurgery for OCD; however, subtle differences do occur on the Wisconsin Card Sorting Test that assesses frontal lobe function.[92, 93, 146]

These results suggest that 25 to 30 percent of OCD patients who previously were refractory to multiple treatment interventions may improve with neurosurgery. However, all reported studies have been uncontrolled and have included relatively few patients. With these issues in mind, further research is needed before neurosurgery can be considered anything but a last-resort option.

Electroconvulsive Therapy (ECT)

ECT is used to elicit a grand mal seizure by controlled electrical stimulation. Although ECT is a highly effective treatment for severe depression, it is rarely effective for OCD.[149]

ECT is typically ineffective for most OCD patients, although there are isolated reports suggesting that it may be beneficial for some patients.[150] As a result, ECT should only be considered for OCD patients who: a) have severe, co-existing depression complicated by psychotic features or suicidal ideation; or b) have failed to respond to standard treatment interventions, including medication and behavioral therapy.[97, 115]

How Effective Are Medications vs. Behavior Therapy in Treating OCD?

In the ongoing debate about the efficacy of medications versus psychotherapy, these factors are critical:

- Early (acute) treatment results and short-term gains

- Follow-up studies and relapse rates

- Willingness of patients to take medications (with sometimes intolerable side effects) versus ability to comply with the demands of exposure treatment

- Cost considerations

- Type of symptoms (e.g., limited data on effectiveness of behavior therapy for those with only obsessions or atypical compulsions)

Education and information about OCD and effective treatments represents one of the most important components in maximizing a successful treatment.

OCD treatment outcome researchers have primarily compared the results of behavior therapy (especially Exposure and Response Prevention) with SRI medication. They have found that both SRI medication and Exposure and Response Prevention yield gains in short-term treatment of six months or less. Exposure and Response Prevention studies have found that 90 percent of clients were at least moderately improved after treatment. At the time of follow-up evaluation (months to several years), 76 percent remained improved.[30] SRI medication is similarly effective with 65 to 80 percent of patients improving immediately after treatment.[25, 116]

However, follow-up studies with drug therapy are not as promising as those on behavioral therapy. Several studies indicate as many as 90 percent of medication responders relapse within four weeks of discontinuing SRI medication.[117] Therefore, researchers consider behavior therapy as the first-line option for treating OCD and find it particularly essential as an add-on treatment for patients taking medications, especially those considering discontinuation of medication.[97]

This extremely high relapse rate, coupled with sometimes-intolerable side effects, often make medication less desirable than Exposure and Response Prevention. SRI antidepressants are valuable for clients who either refuse or fail to respond to exposure treatment. Conversely, exposure therapy may help clients who are taking medications maintain their treatment gains or may be preferable to experiencing some side effects. Therefore, combining SRI antidepressants and Exposure and Response Prevention seems to facilitate one another with many clients and may be the best available treatment for most people with OCD.[30]

Initially, medications are more cost-effective than psycho-therapy. However, the higher relapse rates associated with OCD medication treatment may necessitate long-term and perhaps even life-long medication treatment or added behavior therapy to prevent relapse. Therefore, though OCD medication treatment is less expensive in the short-term, behavioral therapy may be more cost-effective over time.

Several additional factors should be considered when comparing results of medication versus behavior therapy for OCD. These factors suggest some reasons why the results achieved with behavior therapy exceed those attained with medication treatment in OCD. For example, subjects with primary cleaning or checking rituals are over-represented in OCD behavioral therapy studies, and extraordinary success rates are often achieved when such patients receive behavior therapy. However, it remains controversial whether the results from behavioral therapy studies are applicable to the majority of people with OCD. In particular, there is very limited data concerning the success rate for behavior therapy in OCD subjects who have only obsessions or exhibit less common compulsions such as hoarding, counting, or symmetry/completeness.[30, 114, 115, 151]

In contrast, patients with a wide array of OCD symptoms, including the more difficult-to-treat symptoms of hoarding, counting, and perfectionism, are routinely included in medication studies. This may explain in part the reduced, long-term success rate associated with medication treatment.

With all these issues in mind, combined medication and behavioral therapy, which is currently receiving much research attention, probably represents the most effective treatment for OCD. Recent research results confirming that the same biochemical changes occur after either medication or behavioral therapy, further reinforce this approach.[21, 22]

Therapy Notes
From the Desk
of Pat Owen

Amy seems much improved with treatment. Depression is low, and suicidal thoughts are gone. Her insomnia may be a drug side effect — will try reducing dose to manage this. Taper off medications in six months if progress is stable. However, monitor suicidal ideation and reinstate medication if suicidal thoughts recur. Progress on hierarchy exposures is generally good. Husband helpful, but she's doing most of the work. Still needs exposure to symbols of the devil that bother her. Begin to space out sessions after two more visits — recheck Y-BOCS scores then, and plan for relapse prevention. Very motivated client.

Appendix A: Assessment Measures

OCD assessment measures include:

- Client-Rated Self-Report Instruments
- Structured Interviews
- Psychometric Assessments

Client-Rated Self-Report Instruments

Client-rated, self-report instruments include:

- Maudsley Obsessional Compulsive Inventory (MOCI)
- Padua Inventory (PI)
- Compulsive Activity Checklist (CAC)
- Yale-Brown Obsessive Compulsive Checklist & Scale-Self-Report form (Y-BOCS) (See pages 84-85.)

MOCI

Created in 1977, the MOCI remains a commonly used, self-report measure of OCD symptoms.[152] The inventory consists of 30 true/false questions. It yields a total score and six subscale scores including:

- Checking
- Cleaning
- Slowness
- Doubting
- Conscientiousness
- Ruminating

Studies show that this assessment is highly sensitive to treatment effects. It provides a *reliable* measure of symptom severity before, during, and after treatment. The MOCI assesses washing and checking compulsions, which are the most common, but does not assess other important compulsions such as hoarding and covert or mental rituals.[20] Unfortunately, because of this emphasis on overt compulsions, those who suffer with atypical symptoms (e.g., mental rituals) may not score in the pathological range despite debilitating symptoms.[19] A revised version that corrects these problems is currently being developed.

The following client-rated. self-report assessments are not as comprehensive in assessing OCD symptoms as the PI. MOCI. or CAC or Y-BOCS:

- *Symptom Checklist-90 (SCL-90) – Only one very brief subscale among many measures obsessive or compulsive symptoms.*

- *Leyton Obsessional Inventory (LOI) – Provides a narrow focus on OCD. mostly on contamination/cleaning symptoms.*

reliable – the extent to which a test yields consistent results when utilized repeatedly under similar conditions

The MOCI is valid and reliable. but it is limited by its narrow scope of obsessive and compulsive symptoms, focusing on cleaning and checking.

Padua Inventory (PI)

Published by Italian researchers in 1988, the PI consists of 60 items that assess common obsessive and compulsive symptoms and the degree to which they interfere with daily functioning.[153] Each item is rated on a five-point scale and measures the degree of disturbance brought on by a thought or behavior. The scores range from 0 (not at all) to 4 (very much). The total score range is from 0 to 240. The PI measures symptoms using four scales:

1. **Contamination** — The Contamination Scale contains typical washing and cleaning compulsions. It includes statements, such as "I avoid public telephones because I am afraid of contagion or disease."

2. **Checking** — The Checking Scale measures typical checking and repeating compulsions. A representative statement is: "I check and recheck gas and water taps and light switches after turning them off."

3. **Mental Control** — The Mental Control scale measures ability to control, suppress, or ignore obsessive thoughts and includes an assessment of certainty or doubt. Statements include, "I invent doubts and problems about most of the things I do," "I worry about remembering completely unimportant things and make an effort not to forget them," or "When I start thinking of certain things, I become obsessed with them."

4. **Impulses** — The Impulses scale assesses concern about harming others due to carelessness, lack of preparation, loss of self-control, or inability to provide a safe environment.

The PI is one of the most comprehensive assessments of OCD, offering more clinical utility due to the inclusion of significantly more items than in the MOCI. The PI has demonstrated satisfactory reliability and *validity*.[19] As a result, it is increasingly utilized in research studies.[19]

validity — the extent to which the test actually measures what it claims to measure

Compulsive Activity Checklist (CAC)

Developed in 1975, the CAC was originally an interviewer-administered schedule but now exists in both self-report and clinician-rated formats. [154]

82

The original clinician-rated CAC was developed to assess the extent to which obsessive and compulsive symptoms interfere with everyday activities. Each of the 62 items lists a ritualized activity such as washing, dressing, or using electrical appliances that is scored on a four-point scale, ranging from 0 (performing within normal limits) to 3 (complete impairment). Impairment is scored using four criteria:

Criteria for "normal" or "odd" behavior are left to the clinician's judgment.

1. Frequency
2. Duration
3. Avoidance
4. Oddity of behavior

A 38-item, self-report version of the CAC demonstrates validity, reliability, and sensitivity to treatment change.[154] This version also demonstrates adequate *discriminability* of people with obsessions and compulsions from people with other conditions.

discriminability – ability to distinguish between obsessive-compulsive disorder and non-OCD behaviors

Currently, the PI and MOCI are more commonly used than the CAC for two reasons. First, the CAC measures current behaviors and activities without linking them to obsessions. Because the CAC has not been commonly used in clinical and research settings, comparison with other clinical OCD samples is not readily available.

Structured Interviews

Structured interviews include:

- Structured Clinical Interview for the DSM-IV (SCID)
- Anxiety Disorders Interview Schedule-Revised (ADIS-R)
- Yale-Brown Obsessive Compulsive Scale & Symptom Checklist-Interview version (Y-BOCS)

Structured Clinical Interview for the DSM-IV (SCID) and Anxiety Disorders Interview Schedule-Revised (ADIS-R)

Many clinicians use structured interview techniques to diagnose OCD in clinical or community samples, especially the SCID and the ADIS-R.[155, 156] These interviews are often time-consuming and difficult to use in clinical practice and tend to be used mainly for research purposes.

Trained interviewers use the SCID and the ADIS to ensure a structured and consistent format for identifying the presence of psychiatric symptoms. Both instruments require an hour or less to administer the OCD section, and they reliably diagnose OCD according to DSM criteria. However, in each case, more time is required to complete the entire interview for all psychiatric disorders.[19]

No data exists comparing these two interviews. Clinicians generally prefer the ADIS because it more thoroughly details and quantifies OCD symptoms, especially insight into obsessive fears, resistance, and avoidance. Both instruments may be used *formally* to diagnose OCD or *informally* during initial clinical interviews to identify major OCD symptoms.

formally – *strictly following the order of questions*

informally – *the evaluator asks only those questions believed to pertain to that individual client*

Yale-Brown Obsessive Compulsive Scale (Y-BOCS)

Perhaps the most useful structured interview tool for clinicians to use in rating a client's obsessive and compulsive behavior is the Yale-Brown Obsessive Compulsive Scale (Y-BOCS), published in 1989.[157] To use the Y-BOCS, the clinician initially reads definitions and examples of obsessions and compulsions to the client. Then, the clinician asks about past or current experience with 36 specific obsessions and 23 specific rituals on a checklist, containing the following general categories.[19]

The Y-BOCS has become the "gold standard" for assessing OCD in treatment outcome studies.[19]

- Aggressive/harming
- Contamination
- Sexual
- Hoarding/saving
- Religious
- Symmetry/exactness
- Somatic
- Miscellaneous

Assessment of the client's answers is far more comprehensive with the Y-BOCS than with other OCD instruments. Ten questions (five concerning obsessions and five about compulsions), assess OCD symptom severity. OCD obsessions and compulsions are each assessed in terms of five aspects of OCD pathology:

1. Time spent
2. Interference
3. Distress
4. Resistance
5. Perceived control

Each of the 10 questions are scored on a scale from 0 (no symptoms) to 4 (extreme symptoms). The totals are added to yield a total score ranging from 0 to 40. Scores of 8-15 are considered mild, 16-23 moderate, 24-31 severe, and 32-40-extreme.

"For treatment outcome research, the Y-BOCS appears to be the best available instrument in terms of range of obsessive-compulsive symptoms assessed, reliability, validity, and sensitivity to treatment effects."[20]

Two modified versions of the Y-BOCS have been developed, a self-report and a computer-administered version. They both reduce the time and ultimately the costs associated with this comprehensive assessment.

*   **The self-report version of the Y-BOCS** is very similar to the original Y-BOCS, but allows clients to fill out the questionnaire on their own. This approach reduces costs because administration does not require the presence of the clinician.

*   **The computer-assisted, telephone administration of the Y-BOCS** utilizes digitized human speech over the phone to provide a reliable, low-cost method capable of generating immediate scores. Unfortunately, this approach requires clients to be comfortable using a computer and to use the clinic's computer to complete the interview.

The original Y-BOCS demonstrated very good *criterion-related validity* as well as *convergent validity*. The computer-administered and self-report versions also perform well in these areas, but require further evaluation.[20] The Y-BOCS is most useful for quantifying the level or severity of obsessive compulsive symptoms and measuring response to treatment.[20] Its two main weaknesses are:

criterion-related validity – the extent to which a measure of an attribute demonstrates an association with some independent or external indicator of that same attribute

convergent validity – the relationship of a test to independent measures of the same trait

1. It is designed to assess OCD symptom severity, not to diagnose the disorder.

2. It is time consuming, requiring approximately 45 minutes to one hour to administer.

85

Psychometric Assessments

Psychometric assessments include:

- The Minnesota Multiphasic Personality Inventory (MMPI-2)

- Rorschach Inkblot Test

- Thematic Apperception Test (TAT)

- Wechsler Adult Intelligence Scale-Revised (WAIS-R)

MMPI-2

psychopathology – *psychological and behavioral dysfunction occurring in mental disorders*

The MMPI-2 is widely used in clinical settings to assess personality as well as *psychopathology*.[158, 159] Scores from the lengthy, true-false test enable clinicians to profile test-taking attitudes, clinical problems, and specific scale scores. Scale 7 of the MMPI specifically measures:

- Obsessions
- Compulsions
- Anxiety or worrying
- Unreasonable fears
- Guilt feelings

psychasthenia – *a term for a disorder characterized by anxiety, obsessions and fixed ideas*

T-Scores – *standardized scores based on a scale of 1 to 100 with 50 as the mean*

This scale is a good indicator of general maladjustment, tension, anxiety, and ruminative self-doubt.[159] Elevated scores on this *psychasthenia* scale (*T-scores* above 80) suggest that the individual may have traits suggestive of OCD, including being anxious, tense, worried, and apprehensive. Moderately high scores (T-scores between 60 and 80) suggest that the individual has many fears; is nervous, jittery, indecisive and may be lacking in self-confidence.

MMPI scales:
1. *Hypochondriasis*
2. *Depression*
3. *Hysteria*
4. *Psychopathic Deviate*
5. *Masculinity/Femininity*
6. *Paranoia*
7. *Psychasthenia*
8. *Schizophrenia*
9. *Hypomania*
0. *Social Introversion*

The three most common profile combinations correlated with OCD are:

1. The client's highest scores are on Scale 7 (psychasthenia scale) and on either Scale 8 (schizophrenia) or scale 2 (depression) (i.e., 7-8/8-7 or 7-2/2-7).

2. The client has elevated scores on all three scales (i.e., 7-8-2). This profile (possibly the most predictive of OCD) reflects individuals who are self-analytic and

inclined toward catastrophic expectations and a sense of hopelessness.

3. The client has an elevated score on only Scale 7 (psychasthenia). Such people also tend to have either a high score on Scale 3 (obsessiveness), reflecting difficulties making decisions and rumination, or on Scale 5 (health concerns), indicating concerns about cleanliness and health.

Scores on the MMPI/MMPI-2 are not specific enough for establishing a diagnosis of OCD. Clinicians must consider other information when evaluating results.

Rorschach Inkblot Test

The Rorschach Inkblot Test consists of 10 cards with randomly created inkblots, some in monochrome and some in color.[160] The clinician shows the cards to clients one at a time, recording and scoring their answers. This test is a *"projective" measure of personality*, revealing information that can be helpful in diagnosis and treatment planning.

The most widely used system for scoring and interpreting responses to the Rorschach test is the Exner Method.[160,161] This system allows the clinician to determine how unusual a particular score is for a particular client. It also contains useful indices to help identify OCD-related traits. For example, Exner's Obsessive Style Index (OBS) utilizes five key indicators from Rorschach's results. Individuals who score in certain ways on these indicators often possess similar tendencies or characteristics to people with OCD. However, the score by itself cannot be directly equated with OCD.

Individuals with OCD tend to show certain behaviors during the administration of the test to a greater degree than non-OCD individuals.[161] For example, they may express a great deal of doubt, criticize the blots and their own responses, or show concern about the symmetry of the cards. Because the Rorschach is both time and labor intensive, it is an inefficient tool for diagnosis. However, this test may be especially useful for developing treatment plans and understanding a client's therapy progress because it enhances insight into the nature of the individual's personality style and illustrates the way they process information.

"projective" measure of personality – as measured by the Rorschach, the stimuli or inkblots are assumed to be neutral; they were created randomly and have no specific shape or function. Shapes, movement, and other elements of the pictures that clients see in the blots are a product of the client's own experiences and perceptual orientation projected on the cards

---

Thematic Apperception Test (TAT)

The TAT, like the Rorschach, is a projective test that presents clients with a series of ambiguous black & white pictures. [162] Clients are asked to make up a story about the picture. Although the TAT is an inefficient tool for diagnosing OCD, individuals with OCD may show certain tendencies during test administration. For example, they may get bogged down in details and use *pedantic wordings,* at the expense of creating a logical story line . Information gained from the TAT about how clients view themselves and their interpersonal relationships may help clinicians understand the client and develop treatment plans.

pedantic wordings –
wordings that are overly
detailed or precise

Wechsler Adult Intelligence Scale-Revised (WAIS-R)

The WAIS-R, like many other intelligence tests, was developed to:[163]

- Measure intellectual potential
- Determine ability to process language
- Assess functional integrity of the brain
- Obtain clinically relevant information on decision-making capacity

The purpose of the WAIS-R is not to provide diagnostic information; instead, it estimates an individual's overall *IQ.*[161] Clients with OCD tend to score higher than normal on overall IQ, especially verbal IQ.

IQ – Intelligence Quotient,
a measure of intelligence.
Scores between 90 and
110 are considered
"average"

Individuals with OCD are likely to excel in perceptual skill subtests. They may also do quite well on Vocabulary and Comprehension subtests because of their care and precision. However, their inability to switch or adapt to a new grouping strategy can penalize their score on the Similarities subtests.

Appendix B: Recommended Resources on Obsessive Compulsive Disorder

---

Books for Professionals

Hollander, E., & Stein, D.J. (Eds.) (1997). Obsessive-compulsive disorders. New York: Marcel Dekker, Inc. — *An excellent compendium of chapters that cover several theoretical models for OCD, especially biological models, as well as pharmacological, behavioral and other forms of treatment for this disorder.*

Jenike, M.A., Baer, L., & Minichiello, W.E. (Eds.) (1998). Obsessive-compulsive disorders: Practical management. St. Louis: Mosby. — *This is probably the most comprehensive of edited volumes on OCD with 30 chapters and several appendices covering clinical symptoms, spectrum disorders, pathophysiology and assessment, and several forms and formats for biological and psychosocial treatment.*

Steketee, G. (1993). Treatment of obsessive compulsive disorder. New York: Guilford. — *This is a clinical guide with the first five chapters covering information about OCD and the next six giving step-by-step instructions to clinicians for assessment and behavioral treatment of obsessions and compulsions. Appendices provide useful measures and forms.*

Swinson, R.P., Antony, M.M., Rachman, S., & Richter, M.A. (Eds.) (1998). Obsessive-compulsive disorder: Theory, research and treatment. New York: Guilford. — *An excellent, edited book with chapters written by experts in the field. Topics covered include psychopathology and theoretical perspectives, assessment, biological and psychological treatments, and spectrum disorders.*

Articles on OCD Treatment

Freeston, M.H., Rhéaume, J., & Ladouceur, R. (1996). Correcting faulty appraisals of obsessional thoughts. Behaviour Research and Therapy, 34, 433-446.

Van Oppen, P., & Arntz, A. (1994). Cognitive therapy for obsessive-compulsive disorder. Behaviour Research and Therapy, 32, 79-87.

Both journal articles discuss how to conduct cognitive therapy in detail for clinicians interested in providing this treatment for OCD clients, illustrating specific techniques.

OCD Consensus Treatment Guidelines (1997). Journal of Clinical Psychiatry, 58 (4).

89

Therapy Manuals

Kozak, M.J. & Foa, G.B. (1997). <u>Mastery of obsessive compulsive disorder: A cognitive-behavioral approach.</u> San Antonio, TX: The Psychological Corporation.
— *A therapist guide and client workbook.*

Steketee, G. (1998). <u>Overcoming obsessive compulsive disorder: Behavioral and cognitive therapy.</u> Oakland, CA: New Harbinger.
— *A therapist protocol and client manual.*

Books for OCD Sufferers and Their Families

Baer, L. (1991). <u>Getting control</u>. Lexington, MA: Little, Brown & Co.

Foa, E.B., & Wilson, R. (1991). <u>Stop obsessing</u>! New York: Bantam.

Steketee, G., & White, K. (1990). <u>When once is not enough</u>. Oakland, CA: New Harbinger Press.

Neziroglu, F. & Yaryura-Tobias, J.A. (1991). <u>Over and over again: Understanding Obsessive Compulsive Disorder.</u> Lexington, MA: Lexington Books.

These self-help books provide very clear descriptions of OCD and step-by-step methods for assessing and treating this condition using behavior therapy techniques.

Glossary

A

anal-retentiveness — *individual derives pleasure from cleanliness and order*

anal stage — *the second stage in Freud's theory of psychosexual development concerned with the retention and expulsion of waste*

anal wishes — *desires based on regression to the anal stage, such as excessive need to maintain order and cleanliness*

Anoxia — *brain cell death resulting from interruption of oxygen supply to the brain*

antibodies — *complex protein molecules created specifically to destroy organisms deemed to be dangerous*

augmenting — *adding in another medication to enhance therapeutic benefits*

Aversion Relief — *the process of punishing behavior followed by the ending of the punishment when the person stops the undesired thoughts or behaviors*

B

basal ganglia — *brain area containing several structures, including the caudate nucleus, putamen, and substantia nigra, the primary function of which is to initiate and control body movement*

C

capsulotomy — *removal of the front part of the internal capsule of the brain, which contains nerves that connect the cerebral cortex to the basal ganglia*

CAT scans — *computerized axial tomography; computer-assisted x-rays*

caudate nucleus — *a basal ganglia component involved in the voluntary movement control and filtering and refining input from other parts of the brain*

cingulotomy — *removal of the mid-line fold in the outer layer of both sides of the brain, which contains neural pathways from the cortex to the inner brain*

controlled research studies — *research studies in which the various treatments in the study are regulated so that causal factors can be unambiguously identified*

convergent validity — *the relationship of a test to independent measures of the same trait*

corrective emotional experience — *when a client re-experiences with the therapist an old, chronic conflicting pattern of behavior, such as extreme dependency, and the therapeutic relationship allows for a different healing outcome to the old pattern of behavior*

criterion-related validity — *the extent to which a measure of an attribute demonstrates an association with some independent or external indicator of that same attribute*

D

discriminability — *ability to distinguish between obsessive-compulsive disorder and non-OCD behaviors*

displacement — *having or expressing a feeling toward someone or something other than where it belongs*

E

ego strength — *self-confidence, resourcefulness, stability, and ability to cope with problems and stresses in their life situations*

Encephalitis — *infection of the brain*

etiology — *the cause of a disorder*

Exposure and Response Prevention therapy — *the client confronts obsessional cues and is prevented from performing compulsions*

F

formally — strictly following the order of questions

fraternal — dizygotic or non-identical twin derived from separate eggs and possessing different genetic characteristics

G

gene — DNA sequence located at a specific site on a chromosome that codes for a certain characteristic(s); the biological basis of heredity

genetic — hereditary

genetic link — tendency for genes that code for separate characteristics to be inherited together even though found at different locations on the chromosomes

group cohesiveness — the degree to which group members work together for the benefit of each other and the group as a whole

H

habituation — gradual, naturally occurring reduction of anxiety or discomfort over time, if exposure is maintained

half-life — the time required to eliminate 50 percent of a medication from the body

hallucinations — false sensory perceptions

hypnotics — medications that promote sleep

hypothalamus — a small brain structure critically involved in survival functions, such as temperature regulation, heart rate, blood pressure, feeding behavior, water intake, and emotional and sexual behavior

I

Imagined Exposure — exposure to the feared stimuli through the use of mental imagery

Imagined Flooding — a clinical procedure where the therapist helps the client repeatedly

visualize being exposed to a certain obsessive cue without ritualizing until that cue or situation no longer evokes anxiety or discomfort

inappropriate affect — mood incongruent with context of a situation

informally — the evaluator asks only those questions believed to pertain to that individual client

insight — self-awareness or self-understanding of the underlying dynamics of one's actions

interpreting — the clinician reflects to the client hypotheses regarding the connection between unconscious material and current or conscious feelings or behavior

In-vivo Exposure — exposure to the actual anxiety-eliciting stimulus, such as a garbage can

IQ — Intelligence Quotient, a measure of intelligence. Scores between 90 and 110 are considered "average"

irrational beliefs — false perceptions of reality based on exaggerated expectations

isolation — disconnecting impulses and resulting feelings from the original memories associated with them

L

limbic system — brain region involved in smell, automatic behaviors, and emotions that surrounds the midbrain and has extensive connections with the thalamus and brain stem

loosening of associations — an individual's speech slips off the track from one topic to another

M

meta-analysis — a study of the collective findings of many individual outcome studies to give an overall level of effectiveness for a certain type of treatment

modeling — *clinician demonstrates exposure for the client*

monozygotic — *derived from the same fertilized egg and identical genetic make-up*

MRI — *Magnetic Resonance Imaging*

N

negative automatic thoughts — *immediate interpretations about the meaning of obsessive thoughts*

neurons — *nerve cells consisting of cell bodies or soma, axons*

neurotransmitters — *chemical messengers that transmit signals from one nerve cell to another to elicit physiological responses*

O

over-valued ideation — *belief that obsessive fears are realistic*

P

paradoxical intention – *a technique where the therapist instructs the client to do more of the obsessions or compulsions*

pedantic wordings — *wordings that are overly detailed or precise*

PET — *Positron Emission Tomography*

positive transference — *the client recalls and relives pleasant experiences, feelings, and memories from the past as if they were occurring in the present*

Post-Encephalitic Parkinsonism — *rigidity, tremor, and abnormally slow movements that develops as a result of encephalitis lethargica or "sleeping sickness"*

post-synaptic neuron — *area lying adjacent to the nerve terminal that contains the post-synaptic receptors*

pre-synaptic — *neuronal area proximal to the synapse*

prognosis — *outcome in the future*

Progressive Supranuclear Palsy — *weakness and paralysis caused by brain cell deterioration in the cerebral cortex, basal ganglia, and other upper motor areas*

projective measure of personality — *as measured by the Rorschach, the stimuli or inkblots are assumed to be neutral; they were created randomly and have no specific shape or function. Shapes, movement, and other elements of the pictures that clients see in the blots are a product of the client's own experiences and perceptual orientation projected on the cards*

psychasthenia — *a term for a disorder characterized by anxiety, obsessions and fixed ideas*

psychometric tests — *tests which measure psychological factors such as personality, intelligence, beliefs, fears*

psychopathology — *psychological and behavioral dysfunction occurring in mental disorders*

R

reaction formation — *the process through which unacceptable feelings or impulses are controlled by behaving directly opposite of them (e.g., someone who cleans compulsively to avoid the unconscious feeling of being unacceptable or dirty*

receptors — *membrane-bound protein molecules with a highly specific shape that facilitates complimentary binding by neurotransmitters or drugs*

regression — *the act of going back in one's mind to an earlier period or an earlier way of functioning*

reliable — *the extent to which a test yields consistent results when utilized repeatedly under similar conditions*

Response Prevention — *deliberate blocking of overt and mental rituals and obsessive avoidance behaviors*

S

satiation — *a clinical procedure where the therapist has the client verbalize ruminations while the therapist encourages the client through the use of verbal prompts*

Schizotypal Personality Disorder — *a personality disorder characterized by markedly eccentric and erratic thought, speech, and behavior and a tendency to withdraw from other people*

sedatives — *medications that help suppress anxiety by calming agitation and relaxing muscles*

serotonergic medication — *medications that specifically effect the neurotransmitter serotonin*

serotonin hypothesis — *the theory that impaired serotonin neurotransmission in the brain is related to the OCD development*

Social Phobia — *a disorder characterized by episodes of panic anxiety in oscial settings due to excessive concern about public embarassment or possible adverse scrutiny*

Socratic questioning — *posing a series of questions to force the client to defend irrational beliefs, such as: "What evidence do you have to support that idea? What's the likelihood of such an outcome? What are other possible explanations?"*

SPECT — *Single Photon Emission Computerized Tomography*

state like — *a current, non-permanent condition*

Subjective Units of Discomfort scale (SUDs) — *a scale ranging from 10-100 with 10 being the least anxiety provoking and 100 being the most anxiety provoking. The SUDs scoring system allows the client to express exactly how upsetting or distressing certain stimuli are in comparison to other anxiety experiences*

Sydenham's Chorea — *condition triggered by rheumatic infection of the brain and characterized by involuntary, irregular muscle movements involving the face, neck, and limbs*

synaptic cleft — *gap between neurons*

Systematic Desensitization — *a clinical technique that pairs relaxation with imagery of anxiety-eliciting situations*

T

thalamus — *brain area with multiple connections to other brain regions. It primarily functions as a relay station for body sensations, including pain and temperature*

thought insertion — *the belief that some other being is placing thoughts in one's mind*

Thought Stopping — *disrupting thoughts by having the person use the word or image "Stop!" immediately following the thought to be prevented*

Tourette's Syndrome — *neurological disorder characterized by semi-voluntary motor tics and vocalizations*

trait like — *an enduring condition*

T-Scores — *standardized scores based on a scale of 1 to 100 with 50 as the mean*

U

undoing — *either mentally replaying or physically performing an act in an attempt to have a more acceptable ending to a previously unacceptable outcome*

V

validity — *the extent to which the test actually measures what it claims to measure*

Bibliography

1.   American Psychiatric Association (1994). Diagnostic and statistical manual of mental disorders (4th ed.). Washington, DC: American Psychiatric Association.

2.   Riggs, D.S., and Foa, E.B. (1993). Obsessive compulsive disorder. In D.H. Barlow (Ed.). Clinical handbook of psychological disorders. New York: Guilford.

3.   Rachman, S.J. (1985). An overview of clinical and research issues in obsessional-compulsive disorders. In M. Mavissakalia, S.M. Turner, and L. Michelson (Eds.). Obsessive-compulsive disorder: Psychological and pharmacological treatment. New York: Plenum Press.

4.   Morrison, J. (1995). DSM-IV made easy: The clinician's guide to diagnosis. New York: Guilford Press.

5.   Koran, L.M., Thienemann, M.L., and Davenport, R. (1966). Quality of life for patients with obsessive-compulsive disorder. American Journal of Psychiatry, 153, 783-788.

6.   Steketee, G. (1997). Disability and family burden in obsessive compulsive disorder. Canadian Journal of Psychiatry, 42, 919-928.

7.   Greist, J.H., and Jefferson, J.W. (1995). Obsessive compulsive disorder. In G.O. Gabbard (Ed.) Treatment of Psychiatric Disorders (2nd ed.) (pp. 1477-1498).

8.   Stanley, M.A., and Turner, S.M. (1995). Current status of pharmacological and behavioral treatment of obsessive-compulsive disorder. Behavior Therapy, 26, 163-186.

9.   Foa, E.B., and Kozak, M.J. (1986). Emotional processing of fear: Exposure to corrective information. Psychological Bulletin, 99, 20-35.

10. Cottraux, J. and Gerard, D. (1998). Neuroimaging and neuroanatomical issues in OCD. In R. Swinson, M. Antony, S. Rachman and M. Richter (Eds.) OCD: Theory, Research, and Treatment (pp. 154-180). New York: The Guilford Press.

11. Cummings, J.L. and Cunningham, K. (1992). Obsessive-compulsive disorder in Huntington's disease. Biological Psychiatry, 31(3), 263-70.

12. Rauch, S.L. and Jenike, M.A. (1993). Neurobiological models of obsessive-compulsive disorder. Psychosomatics, 34(1), 20-32.

13. Allen, A., Leonard, H. and Swedo, S. (1995). Case study: A new infection-triggered, autoimmune subtype of pediatric OCD and Tourette's syndrome. Journal of the American Academy of Child & Adolescent Psychiatry, 34(3), 307-311.

14. Kettle, P. and Marks, I. (1986). Neurological factors in obsessive-compulsive disorder: two case reports and a review of the literature. British Journal of Psychiatry, 149, 315-319.

15. Miguel-Filho, E. (1995). [Obsessive-compulsive disorder and the basal ganglia]. Arq-Neuropsiquiatr, 53(4), 858-9.

16. Modell, J., Mountz, J., Curtis, G. and Greden, J. (1989). Neurophysiologic dysfunction in basal ganglia/limbic striatal and thalamocortical circuits as a pathogenetic mechanism of obsessive-compulsive disorder. Journal of Neuropsychiatry, 1, 27-36.

17. Steketee, G. S. (1993). Treatment of obsessive-compulsive disorder. New York: Guilford.

18. Steketee, G., and Pruyn, N. A. (1998). Families of individuals with OCD. In R. P. Swinson, M. M. Antony, S. J. Rachman, and M. A. Richters (Eds.) Obsessive compulsive disorder: Theory, research, and treatment. New York: Guilford.

19. Steketee, G. (1994). Behavioral assessment and treatment planning with obsessive compulsive disorder: A review emphasizing clinical application. Behavior Therapy, 25, 613-633.

20. Taylor, S. (1995). Assessment of obsessions and compulsions: reliability, validity, and sensitivity to treatment effects. Clinical Psychology Review, 15, 261-296.

21. Baxter, L.R., Schwartz, J.M., Bergman, K.S., Szubba, M.P., Guze, B.H., Mazziotta, J.C., Alazraki, A., Selin, C.E., Ferng, H.K., Munford, P., and Phelps, M.E. (1992). Caudate glucose metabolic rate changes with both drug and behavior therapy for obsessive-compulsive disorder. Archives of General Psychiatry, 49, 681-689.

22. Schwartz, J., Stoessel, P., Baxter, L., Martin, K. and Phelps, M. (1996). Systematic changes in cerebral glucose metabolic rate after successful behavior modification treatment of OCD. Archives of General Psychiatry, 53, 109-113.

23. Foa, E.B., Steketee, G., and Ozarow, B.J. (1985). Behavior therapy with obsessive-compulsives: From theory to treatment. In M. Mavissakalian, S.M. Turner, and L. Michelson (Eds.) Obsessive-compulsive disorder: Psychological and pharmacological treatments. (pp. 49-120). New York: Plenum Press.

24. Meyer, V., Levy, R., and Schnurer, A. (1974). The behavioural treatment of obsessive-compulsive disorders. In H.R. Beech (Ed.) Obsessional states. (pp. 233-258). London: Methuen & Co.

25. Perse, T. (1988). Obsessive-compulsive disorder: A treatment review. Journal of Clinical Psychiatry, 49, 48-55.

26. Emmelkamp, P.M., and Kraanen, J. (1977). Therapist-controlled exposure in vivo versus self-controlled exposure in vivo: A comparison with obsessive-compulsive patients. Behaviour Research and Therapy, 15(6), 491-495.

27. Clark, A., Kirkby, K.C., Daniels, BA., and Marks, I.M. (1998). A pilot study of computer-aided vicarious exposure for obsessive-compulsive disorder: Erratum. Australian & New Zealand Journal of Psychiatry, 32(5), 740.

28. Osgood-Hynes, D.J., Greist, J.H., Marks, I.M., Baer, L., Heneman, S.W., Wenzel, K.W., Manzo, P.A., Parkin, J.R., Spierings, C.J., Dottl, S.L., and Vitse, H.M. (1998). Self-administered psychotherapy for depression using a telephone-accessed computer system plus booklets: An open U.S.-U.K. study. Journal of Clinical Psychiatry, 59(7), 358-365.

29. Greist, J.H. (1990). Treatment of Obsessive-Compulsive Disorder: psychotherapies, drugs, and other somatic treatment. Journal of Clinical Psychiatry, 51, 44-50.

30. Greist, J. (1992). An integrated approach to treatment of obsessive-compulsive disorder. Journal of Clinical Psychiatry, 53(4), 38-41.

31. Beech, H.R., and Vaughn, M. (1978). Behavioral treatment of obsessive states. New York: Wiley.

32. Cooper, J.E., Gelder, M.G., and Marks, I.M. (1965). Results of behavior therapy in 77 psychiatric patients. British Medical Journal, 1, 1222-1225.

33. Abramowitz, J. S. (1997). Effectiveness of psychological and pharmacological treatments for obsessive-compulsive disorder: A quantitative review. Journal of Consulting and Clinical Psychology, 65, 44-52.

34. van Balkom, A. J. M., van Oppen, P., Vermeulen, A. W. A., van Dyck, R., Nauta, M. C. E., & Vorst, H. C. M. (1994). A meta-analysis on the treatment of obsessive-compulsive disorder: A comparison of antidepressants, behavior, and cognitive therapy. Clinical Psychology Review, 14, 359-381.

35. Fritzler, B.K., Hecker, J.E., and Losee, M.C. (1997). Self-directed treatment with minimal therapist contact: Preliminary findings for Obsessive Compulsive Disorder. Behaviour Research and Therapy, 35, 627-631.

36. Hodgson, R.J., Rachman, S., and Marks, I.M. (1972). The treatment of chronic obsessive-compulsive neurosis: Follow-up and further findings. Behaviour Research and Therapy, 10, 181-189.

37. Freeston, M. H., Ladouceur, R., Gagnon, F., Thibodeau, N., Rheaume, J., Letarte, H., & Bujold, A. (1997). Cognitive-behavioral treatment of obsessive thoughts: A controlled study. Journal of Consulting and Clinical Psychology, 65(3), 405-413.

38. Obsessive Compulsive Cognitions Working Group. (1997). Cognitive assessment of obsessive-compulsive disorder. Behaviour Research and Therapy, 35, 667-681.

39. Salkovskis, P.M. (1985). Obsessional compulsive problems: A cognitive behavioral analysis. <u>Behaviour Research and Therapy, 23</u>, 571-583.

40. Rachman, S., Thordarson, D., Shafran, R., and Woody, S. (1995). Perceived responsibility: structure and significance. <u>Behaviour Research and Therapy, 33</u>, 779-784.

41. Freeston, M., Rh'eume, J., & Ladouceur, R. (1996). Correcting faulty appraisals of obsessional thoughts. <u>Behaviour Research and Therapy, 34</u>, 433-446.

42. Ellis, A. (1962). <u>Reason and emotion in psychotherapy</u>. New York: Lyle-Stuart.

43. Warren, R. and Zgourides, G. (1991). <u>Anxiety disorders: A rational emotive perspective.</u> New York: Pergamon.

44. Steketee, G., and Frost, R. O. (in press). Cognitive theory and treatment of obsessive-compulsive disorder. In M. A. Jenike, L. Baer, and W. E. Minichiello (Eds.), <u>Obsessive-compulsive disorders: Practical management</u> (pp. 368-399). St. Louis: Mosby.

45. van Oppen, P., and Arntz, A. (1994). Cognitive therapy for obsessive-compulsive disorder. <u>Behaviour Research and Therapy, 32</u>, 79-87.

46. James, I.A., and Blackburn, I. (1995). Cognitive therapy with obsessive-compulsive disorder. <u>British Journal of Psychiatry, 166</u>, 444-450.

47. Emmelkamp, P.M.G., Visser, S., and Hoekstra, R.J. (1988). Cognitive therapy vs exposure in vivo in the treatment of obsessive-compulsives. <u>Cognitive Therapy and Research, 12</u>, 103-114.

48. Emmelkamp, P.M.G. and Beens, H. (1991). Cognitive therapy with obsessive-compulsive disorder: A comparative evaluation. <u>Behaviour Research and Therapy, 29</u>, 293-300.

49. van Oppen, P., de Haan, E., van Balkom, A.J.L.M., Spinohoven, P., Hoogduin, K., and van Dyck, R. (1995). Cognitive therapy and exposure in vivo in the treatment of obsessive compulsive disorder. <u>Behaviour Research and Therapy, 33</u>, 379-390.

50. Sifneos, P.E. (1985). Short-term dynamic psychotherapy for patients suffering from an Obsessive-Compulsive Disorder. In Mavissakalian, M., Turner, S.M., and Michelson, L. (Eds.) <u>Obsessive-compulsive disorder: Psychological and pharmacological treatment</u>. New York, NY: Plenum Press.

51. Boyarsky, B.K., Perone, L.A., Lee, N.C., and Goodman, W.K. (1991). Current treatment approaches to obsessive-compulsive disorder. <u>Archives of Psychiatric Nursing, 5</u>, 299-306.

52. Kobak, K.A., Rock, A.L., and Greist, J.H. (1995). Group behavior therapy for obsessive- compulsive disorder. <u>The Journal for Specialists in Group Work, 20</u>, 26-32.

53. Fals-Stewart, W., and Lucente, S. (1994). Behavior group therapy with obsessive-compulsives: an overview. <u>International Journal of Group Psychotherapy, 44</u>, 35-51.

54. Black, D.W., and Blum, N.S. (1992). Obsessive-compulsive disorder support groups: the Iowa model. <u>Comprehensive Psychiatry, 33</u>, 65-71.

55. Tynes, L.L., Salins, C., Skiba, W., and Winstead, D.K. (1992). A psychoeducational and support group for obsessive-compulsive disorder patients and their significant others. <u>Comprehensive Psychiatry, 33</u>, 197-201.

56. Van Noppen, B., Steketee, G., McCorkle, B. H., and Pato, M. (1997). Group and multifamily behavioral treatment for obsessive compulsive disorder: A pilot study. <u>Journal of Anxiety Disorders, 11(4)</u>, 431-446.

57. Steketee, G.S., and White, K. (1990). <u>When once is not enough: Help for obsessive compulsives</u>. Oakland, CA: New Harbinger.

58. Baer, L. (1991). <u>Getting Control</u>. Boston: Little, Brown.

59. Foa, E. B., and Wilson, R. (1991). <u>Stop obsessing!</u> New York: Bantam.

60. Espie, C.A. (1986). The group treatment of obsessive compulsive ritualizers: Behavioral management of identified patterns of relapse. <u>Behavioural Psychotherapy, 14</u>, 21-33.

61. Krone, K.P., Himle, J.A., and Nesse, R.M. (1991). A standardized behavioral group treatment program for obsessive-compulsive disorder: Preliminary outcomes. Behaviour Research and Therapy, 29, 627-631.

62. Fals-Stewart, W., Marks, A.P., and Schafer, J. (1993). A comparison of behavioral group therapy and individual behavior therapy in treating obsessive-compulsive disorder. The Journal of Nervous and Mental Disease, 181, 189-193.

63. Chambless, D.L and Steketee, G. (in press). Expressed emotion and behavior therapy outcome for obsessive compulsive and agoraphobia outpatients. Journal of Consulting and Clinical Psychology.

64. Lenane, M., Swedo, S., and Leonard, H. (1990). Psychiatric disorders in first degree relatives of children and adolescents with OCD. Journal of American Academy of Child & Adolescent Psychiatry, 29, 407-412.

65. Rasmussen, S. (1993). Genetic studies of OCD. Annals of Clinical Psychiatry, 5, 241-248.

66. Pauls, D., Alsbrook, J., Goodman, W., Rasmussen, S. and Leckman, J. (1995). A family study of obsessive-compulsive disorder. American Journal of Psychiatry, 152, 76-84.

67. Billett, E., Richter, M. & Kennedy, J. (1998). Genetics of OCD. In R. Swinson, M. Antony, S. Rachman and M. Richter (Eds.), OCD: Theory, Research, and Treatment (pp. 181-206). New York: The Guilford Press.

68. Antony, M., Downie, F. and Swinson, R. (1998). Diagnostic issues and epidemiology in OCD. In R. Swinson, M. Antony, S. Rachman & M. Richter (Eds.) OCD: Theory, Research, and Treatment (pp. 3-32). New York: The Guilford Press.

69. Pigott, T., L'Heureux, F., Dubbert, B., Bernstein, S. and Murphy, D. (1994). Obsessive-compulsive disorder: comorbid conditions, Journal of Clinical Psychiatry, 55(10), 15-27.

70. Rasmussen, S. and Eisen, J. (1992). The epidemiology and clinical features of obsessive-compulsive disorder. Psychiatric Clinics of North America, 15(4), 743-758.

71. Crino, R. and Andrews, G. (1996). OCD and Axis I comorbidity, Journal of Anxiety Disorders, 10, 37-46.

72. Chen, Y. and Dilsaver, S. (1995). Comorbidity for obsessive-compulsive disorder in bipolar and unipolar disorders. Psychiatry Research, 59(1-2), 57-64.

73. Leonard, H., Lenane, M., Swedo, S., Rettew, D., Gershon, E. and Rapaport, J. (1992). Tics and Tourette's syndrome: a two to seven year follow-up of 54 OCD children, American Journal of Psychiatry, 149, 1244-1251.

74. Pauls, D.L., Pakstis, A.J., Kurlan, R., Kidd, K.K., Leckman, J.F., Cohen, D.J., Kidd, J.R., Como, P. and Sparkes, R. (1990). Segregation and linkage analyses of Tourette's syndrome and related disorders, Journal of American Academy of Child & Adolescent Psychiatry, 29(2), 195-203.

75. Goodman, W., McDougle, C., Price, L., Riddle, M., Pauls, D. and Leckman, J. (1990). Beyond the serotonin hypothesis: a role for dopamine in some forms of obsessive-compulsive disorder? Journal of Clinical Psychiatry, 51(8), 36-43.

76. Baxter, L. and Guze, B. (1992). Neuroimaging. In R. Kurlan (Ed.), Handbook of Tourette's syndrome and Related Tic and Behavioral Disorders (pp. 289-304). New York: Dekker.

77. Chase, T., Foster, N., Fenio, P., Brooks, R., Monsi, L., Kessler, R. and Di Chiro, G. (1984). Gilles de la Tourette syndrome: studies with fluorine 18 labeled fluorodeoxyglucose positron emission tomographic methods. Annals of Neurology, 15, 175.

78. Brody, A. and Saxena, S. (1996). Brain imaging in OCD: evidence for the involvement of frontal-subcortical circuitry in the mediation of symptomatology. CNS Spectrums, 1, 27-41.

79. Otto, M.W. (1992). Normal and abnormal information processing. A neuropsychological perspective on obsessive compulsive disorder. Psychiatric Clinics of North America, 15(4), 825-48.

80. Rosenberg, D., Dick, E., O'Hearn, K. and Sweeney, J. (1997). Response-inhibition deficits in obsessive-compulsive disorder: an indicator of dysfunction in frontostriatal circuits. Journal of Psychiatry and Neurosciences, 22(1), 29-38.

81. Stahl, S. (1988). Basal ganglia neuropharmacology and obsessive-compulsive disorder: the obsessive-compulsive disorder hypothesis of basal ganglion dysfunction. Psychopharmacology Bulletin, 24(3), 370-374.

82. Pitman, R., Green, R., Jenike, M. and Mesulam, M. (1987). Animal models of OCD. American Journal of Psychiatry, 143, 1166-1171.

83. Rapaport, J. (1992). An animal model of obsessive-compulsive disorder. Archives of General Psychiatry, 49, 517-521.

84. Yadin, E., Friedman, E. and Bridger, W.H. (1991). Spontaneous alternation behavior: an animal model for obsessive-compulsive disorder? Pharmacology & Biochemistry of Behavior, 40(2), 311-5.

85. Muller, N., Putz, A., Kathmann, N., Lehle, R., Gunther, W. and Straube, A. (1997). Characteristics of obsessive-compulsive symptoms in Tourette's syndrome, obsessive-compulsive disorder, and Parkinson's disease. Psychiatry Research, 70(2), 105-114.

86. Swedo, S., Kilpatrick, K., Schapiro, M., Leonard, H., Cheslow, D. and Rapaport, J. (1991). Antineuronal antibodies in Sydenham's chorea and obsessive-compulsive disorder. Pediatric Research, 29, 364A.

87. Swedo, S., Rapaport, J., Cheslow, D., Leonard, H., Ayoub, E., Hosier, D. and Wald, E. (1989). High prevalence of obsessive-compulsive disorder symptoms in patients with Sydenham's chorea. American Journal of Psychiatry, 146, 246-249.

88. Kiessling, L. S., Marcotte, A. C. and Culpepper, L. (1994). Antineuronal antibodies: tics and obsessive-compulsive symptoms. Journal of Developmental and Behavioral Pediatrics, 15(6), 421-5.

89. Baxter, L., Schwatrz, J., Guze, B., Bergman, K. and Szuba, M. (1990). Neuroimaging in OCD: Seeking the mediating neuroanatomy. In M. Jenike, L. Baer and W. Minichiello (Eds.) OCDs: Theory and Management (pp. 167-188). St. Louis: Mosby YearBook.

90. Rauch, S. and Savage, C. (1997). Neuroimaging and neuropsychology of the striatum. Bridging basic science and clinical practice. Psychiatric Clinics of North America, 20(4), 741-68.

91. Jenike, M., Breiter, H., Baer, L., Kennedy, D., Savage, C., Olivares, M., O'Sullivan, R., Shera, D., Rauch, S., Kenthen, N., Rosen, B., Caviness, V. and Filipek, P. (1996). Cerebral structural abnormalities in OCD. Archives of General Psychiatry, 53, 625-632.

92. Abbruzzese, M., Ferri, S. and Scarone, S. (1995). Wisconsin Card Sorting Test performance in obsessive-compulsive disorder: no evidence for involvement of dorsolateral prefrontal cortex. Psychiatry Research, 58(1), 37-43.

93. Cumming, S., Hay, P., Lee, T. and Sachdev, P. (1995). Neuropsychological outcome from psychosurgery for obsessive-compulsive disorder. Australia & New Zealand Journal of Psychiatry, 29(2), 293-8.

94. Azmitia, E. & Whitaker-Azmitia, P. (1991). Awakening the sleeping giant: anatomy and plasticity of the brain serotonergic system. Journal of Clinical Psychiatry, 52, 4-16.

95. Baumgarten, H. and Grozdanovic, Z. (1995). Psychopharmacology of central serotonergic systems. Pharmacopsychiatry, 28, 73-9.

96. Barr, L., Goodman, W., Price, L., McDougle, C. and Charney, D. (1992). The serotonin hypothesis of obsessive-compulsive disorder: implications of pharmacologic challenge studies. Journal of Clinical Psychiatry, 53(4), 17-28.

97. Jefferson, J.W., Altemus, M., Jenike, M. A., Pigott, T.A., Stein, D. J. and Greist, J.H. (1995). Algorithm for the treatment of obsessive-compulsive disorder (OCD). Psychopharmacology Bulletin, 31(3), 487-490.

98. Murphy, D.L. and Pigott, T.A. (1990). A comparative examination of a role for serotonin in obsessive-compulsive disorder, panic disorder, and anxiety. Journal of Clinical Psychiatry, 51.

99. Pigott, T. (1996). OCD: Where the serotonin-selectivity story begins. Journal of Clinical Psychiatry, 57(6), 11-20.

100. Zohar, J. and Insel, T. (1987). Obsessive-compulsive disorder: psychobiological approaches to diagnosis, treatment, and pathophysiology. Biological Psychiatry, 22, 667-687.

101. Hollander, E., DeCaria, C., Nitescu, A., Gully, R., Suckow, R., Cooper, T., Gorman, J., Klein, D. and Liebowitz, M. (1992). Serotonergic function in obsessive-compulsive disorder: behavioral and neuroendocrine responses to oral m-CPP and fenfluramine in patients and healthy volunteers. Archives of General Psychiatry, 49, 21-28.

102. Barr, L., Goodman, W., McDougle, C., and Delgado, P. (1994). Tryptophan depletion in patients with obsessive-compulsive disorder who respond to serotonin reuptake inhibitors. Archives of General Psychiatry, 51(4), 309-317.

103. Benkelfat, C., Murphy, D., Zohar, J., Hill, J., Grover, G. and Insel, T. (1989). Clomipramine in obsessive-compulsive disorder: further evidence for a serotonergic mechanism of action. Archives of General Psychiatry, 46, 23-28.

104. Hollander, E., DeCaria, C., Nitescu, A., Gorman, J., Klein, D. and Liebowitz, M. (1991). Noradrenergic function in obsessive-compulsive disorder: behavioral and neuroendocrine responses to clonidine and comparison to healthy controls. Psychiatry Research, 137, 161-177.

105. Marazziti, D., Hollander, E., Lensi, P., Ravagli, S. and Cassano, G. (1992). Peripheral markers of serotonin and dopamine function in obsessive-compulsive disorder. Psychiatry Research, 42(1), 41-51.

106. Greist, J., Jefferson, J., Koback, K., Katzelnick, D. and Serlin, R. (1995). Efficacy and tolerability of serotonin transport inhibitors in obsessive-compulsive disorder: A meta-analysis. Archives of General Psychiatry, 52, 53-60.

107. Pigott, T. and Seay, S. (1997). Pharmacotherapy of OCD. International Review of Psychiatry, 9(1), 133-147.

108. Preskorn, S. (1996). Clinical Pharmacology of Selective Serotonin Reuptake Inhibitors. (1st ed.). Caddo, OK: Professional Communications, Inc.

109. DeVane, C. (1992). Pharmacokinetics of the selective serotonin reuptake inhibitors. Journal of Clinical Psychiatry, 53(2), 13-20.

110. Hall, H. and Ogren, S. (1981). Effects of antidepressant drugs on different receptors in the rat brain. European Journal of Pharmacology, (70), 393-407.

111. Frommer, D., Kulig, D., Marx, J. and Rumack, B. (1987). Tricyclic antidepressant overdose. A review. Journal of American Medical Association, 257, 521-526.

112. Keuthen, N., Cyr, P., Ricciardi, J., and Minichiello, W. (1994). Medication withdrawal symptoms in obsessive-compulsive disorder patients treated with paroxetine. Journal of Clinical Psychopharmacology, 14(3), 206-207.

113. Frost, L. and Sal, S. (1995). Shock-like sensations after discontinuation of selective serotonin reuptake inhibitors. American Journal of Psychiatry, 152(5), 810.

114. Goodman, W., McDougle, C., Barr, L. and Price, L. (1993). Biological approaches to the treatment-refractory patient. 1st International OCD Conference Abstracts, Isle of Capri (Italy), 139-140.

115. Jenike, M. and Raush, S. (1994). Managing the patient with treatment-resistant obsessive-compulsive disorder: current strategies. Journal of Clinical Psychiatry, 55, 11-17.

116. Rasmussen, S., Eisen, J. and Pato, M. (1993). Current issues in the pharmacological management of Obsessive-Compulsive Disorder. Journal of Clinical Psychiatry, 54(6), 4-9.

117. Mundo, E., Bareggi, S., Pirola, R., Bellodi, L. and Smeraldi, E. (1997). Long-term pharmacotherapy of obsessive-compulsive disorder: a double-blind controlled study. Journal of Clinical Psychopharmacology, 17(1), 4-10.

118. Pato, M., Hill, J. and Murphy, D. (1990). A clomipramine dosage reduction study in the course of long-term treatment of OCD patients. Psychopharmacology Bulletin, 26, 211-214.

119. Pato, M., Zohar-Kadouch, R., Zohar, J. and Murphy, D. (1988). Return of symptoms after discontinuation of clomipramine in patients with obsessive-compulsive disorder. American Journal of Psychiatry, 145, 1521-1525.

120. Leonard, H., Swedo, S., Lenane, M., Rettew, D., Cheslow, D., Hamburger, S. and Rapaport, J. (1991). A double-blind desipramine substitution during long-term clomipramine treatment in children and adolescents with obsessive-compulsive disorder. Archives of General Psychiatry, 48, 922-927.

121. Tollefson, G., Rampey, A., Potvin, J., and Fenike, M. (1994). A multicenter investigation of fixed-dose fluoxetine in the treatment of obsessive-compulsive disorder. Archives of General Psychiatry, 51(7), 559-567.

122. Greist, J., Chouinard, G., DuBoff, E., and Halaris, A. (1995). Double-blind parallel comparison of three dosages of sertraline and placebo in outpatients with obsessive-compulsive disorder. Archives of General Psychiatry, 52(4), 289-295.

123. Greist, J., Jefferson, J., Kobak, K., and Chouinard, G. (1995). A 1 year double-blind placebo-controlled fixed dose study of sertraline in the treatment of obsessive-compulsive disorder. International Clinical Psychopharmacology, 10(2), 57-65.

124. Wheadon, D., Bushnell, W. and Steiner, M. (1993). *A fixed-dose comparison of 20, 40, or 60 mg. paroxetine to placebo in the treatment of obsessive-compulsive disorder.* Paper presented at the American College of Neuropsychopharmacology (ACNP) Annual Meeting, San Juan, PR.

125. Steiner, M., Bushnell, W., Gergel, I. and Wheadon, D. (1995). *Long-term treatment and prevention of relapse of OCD with paroxetine.* Paper presented at the American Psychiatric Association Annual Meeting, Miami, FL, May 9-12.

126. Rasmussen, S., Goodman, W., Greist, J., Jenike, M., and Kozak, M. (in press). Fluvoxamine in the treatment of OCD: a multi-center double-blind, placebo-controlled study in outpatients. American Journal of Psychiatry.

127. McDougle, C., Goodman, W., Leckman, J., and Lee, N. (1994). Haloperidol addition in fluvoxamine-refractory obsessive-compulsive disorder: A double-blind, placebo-controlled study in patients with and without tics. Archives of General Psychiatry, 51(4), 302-308.

128. McDougle, C. (1994). Risperidone augmentation for refractory OCD. An open study. Journal of Clinical Psychiatry.

129. McDougle, C.J., Fleischmann, R.L., Epperson, C.N., Wasylink, S., Leckman, J.F., and Price, L.H. (1995). Risperidone addition in fluvoxamine-refractory obsessive-compulsive disorder: three cases. Journal of Clinical Psychiatry, 56(11), 526-8.

130. Saxena, S., Wang, D., Bystritsky, A. and Baxter, L.R., Jr. (1996). Risperidone augmentation of SRI treatment for refractory obsessive-compulsive disorder. Journal of Clinical Psychiatry, 57(7), 303-6.

131. Carrasco, J., Hollander, E., Schneier, F. and Liebowitz, M. (1992). Treatment outcome of OCD with comorbid social phobia. Journal of Clinical Psychiatry, 53, 387-391.

132. Jenike, M., Surnam, O., and Cassem, N. (1983). Monoamine oxidase inhibitors in OCD. Journal of Clinical Psychiatry, 44, 131-132.

133. Schulman, K., Walker, S., MacKenzie, S. and Knowles, S. (1989). Dietary restrictions, tyramine, and the uses of monoamine oxidase inhibitors. Journal of Clinical Psychopharmacology, 9, 397-402.

134. Prasad, A. (1985). Efficacy of trazodone as an antiobsessional agent. Pharmacology & Biochemistry of Behavior, 22, 347-348.

135. Pigott, T.A., L'Heureux, F., Rubenstein, C.S., Bernstein, S.E., Hill, J.L. and Murphy, D.L. (1992). A double-blind, placebo controlled study of trazodone in patients with Obsessive-Compulsive Disorder. Journal of Clinical Psychopharmacology, 12(3), 156-162.

136. Rauch, S., O'Sullivan, R. and Jenike, M. (1996). Open Treatment of Obsessive-Compulsive Disorder with Venlafaxine: A Series of Ten Cases. Journal of Clinical Psychopharmacology, 16(1), 81-84.

137. Yaryura-Tobias, J.A. & Neziroglu, F.A., (1995). Venlafaxine in OCD. Archives of General Psychiatry, 52(1), 53-60.

138. Nelson, E.C. (1994). An open-label study of nefazodone in the treatment of depression with and without comorbid obsessive compulsive disorder. Annals of Clinical Psychiatry, 6(4), 249-53.

139. Pato, M.T., Pigott, T.A., Hill, J.L., Grover, G.N., Bernstein, S.E. and Murphy, D.L. (1991). Controlled comparison of buspirone and clomipramine in obsessive-compulsive disorder. American Journal of Psychiatry, 148, 127-129.

140. Hewlett, W., Vinogradov, S. and Agras, W. (1992). Clomipramine, clonazepam, and clonidine treatment of OCD. Journal of Clinical Psychopharmacology, 12, 420-430.

141. Orvin, G. (1967). Treatment of the phobic obsessive-compulsive patient with oxazepam, an improved benzodiazepine compound. Psychosomatics, 8, 278-280.

142. Leonard, H., Topol, D., Bukstein, O., Hindmarsh, D., Allen, A. and Swedo, S. (1994). Clonazepam as an augmenting agent in the treatment of childhood-onset obsessive-compulsive disorder. Journal of the American Academy of Child & Adolescent Psychiatry, 33(6), 792-794.

101

143. Pigott, T., L'Heureux, F., Bernstein, S., Rubenstein, C., Dubbert, B. and Murphy, D. (1992). *A controlled trial of adjuvant clonazepam in clomipramine and fluoxetine treated patients with OCD.* Paper presented at the 145th Annual American Psychiatric Association Meeting, Washington, DC.

144. Simeon, J., Thatte, S. and Wiggins, D. (1990). Treatment of adolescent OCD with a clomipramine-fluoxetine combination. Psychopharmacology Bulletin, 26, 285-290.

145. Browne, M., Horn, E. and Jones, T. (1993). The benefits of clomipramine-fluoxetine combination in OCD. Canadian Journal of Psychiatry, 38, 242-243.

146. Baer, L., Rauch, S., Ballantine, T., and Martuza, R. (1995). Cingulotomy for intractable OCD: prospective long-term follow-up of 18 patients. Archives of General Psychiatry, 52(5), 384-392.

147. Hay, P., Sachdev, P., Cumming, S., Smith, J.S., Lee, T., Kitchener, P. and Matheson, J. (1993). Treatment of obsessive-compulsive disorder by psychosurgery. Acta Psychiatrica Scandinavia, 87(3), 197-207.

148. Mindus, P., Rasmussen, S.A. and Lindquist, C. (1994). Neurosurgical treatment for refractory obsessive-compulsive disorder: implications for understanding frontal lobe function. Journal of Neuropsychiatry and Clinical Neurosciences, 6(4), 467-77.

149. Rabheru, K. and Persad, E. (1997). A review of continuation and maintenance electroconvulsive therapy. Canadian Journal of Psychiatry, 42(5), 476-84.

150. Casey, D. and Davis, M. (1994). Obsessive-compulsive disorder responsive to electroconvulsive therapy in an elderly woman. Southern Medical Journal, 87(8), 862-4.

151. Baer, L. (1993). Behavior therapy for obsessive-compulsive disorder in the office-based practice. Journal of Clinical Psychiatry, 54, 10-15.

152. Hodgson, R.J., and Rachman, S. (1977). Obsessional-compulsive complaints. Behaviour Research and Therapy, 15, 389-395.

153. Sanavio, E. (1988). Obsessions and compulsions: The Padua Inventory. Behaviour Research and Therapy, 26, 169-177.

154. Steketee, G., and Freund, B. (1993). Compulsive Activity Checklist (CAC): Further psychometric analyses and revision. Behavioural Psychotherapy, 21, 13-25.

155. First, M.B., Spitzer, R.L., Gibbon, M., and Williams, J.B.W. (1995). Structured Clinical Interview for DSM-IV Axis I Disorders - Patient Edition (SCID-I/P, Version 2), New York: New York State Psychiatric Institute.

156. DiNardo, P. A., and Barlow, D.H. (1998). Anxiety Disorders Interview Schedule-Revised. Albany, NY: Graywind.

157. Goodman, W.K., Price, L.H., Rasmussen, S.A., Mazure, C., Fleischmann, R.L., Hill, C.L., Heninger, G.R., and Charney, D.S. (1989). The Yale-Brown Obsessive-Compulsive Scale. I. Development, use, and reliability. Archives of General Psychiatry, 46, 1006-1011.

158. Hathaway, S.R., Butcher, J.N., and McKinley, J.C. (1989). Minnesota Multiphasic Personality Inventory-2. Minneapolis, MN: University of Minnesota Press.

159. Butcher, James N. (1990). The MMPI-2 in Psychological Treatment. New York: Oxford University Press.

160. Exner, J.E. (1993). The Rorschach: A comprehensive system; volume 1; basic foundations. Somerset, New Jersey: John Wiley and Sons.

161. Meyer, R..G. (1993). The clinician's handbook: Integrated diagnostics, assessment and intervention in adult and adolescent psychopathology. Boston, MA: Allyn & Bacon.

162. Morgan, C.D., and Murray, H.A. (1938). A method for investigating fantasies. Archives of Neurology and Psychiatry, 34, 289-306.

163. Weschler, D.D. (1981). Manual for the Wechsler Adult Intelligence Scale - Revised. San Antonio: The Psychological Corporation.

Index

We Want Your Opinion!

Comments about the book: _____
Name of Book

_____

_____

_____

_____

Other titles you want Compact Clinicals to offer:

_____

_____

_____

_____

Please provide your name and address in the space below to be placed on our mailing list.

_____

_____

_____

_____

Ordering in three easy steps:
Order 24 hours a day: 1(800)408-8830

1   **Please fill out completely:**

Billing/Shipping Information

Individual/Company   Department/Mail Stop

Street Address/P.O. Box

City, State, Zip

Telephone

2   **Here's what I'd like to order:**

Book Name	Book Qty.	Unit Price	Total
Attention Deficit Hyperactivity Disorder (in Adults and Children) The Latest Assessment and Treatment Strategies		$14.95	
Borderline Personality Disorder The Latest Assessment and Treatment Strategies		$14.95	
Conduct Disorders The Latest Assessment and Treatment Strategies		$14.95	
Major Depressive Disorder The Latest Assessment and Treatment Strategies		$14.95	
Obsessive Compulsive Disorder The Latest Assessment and Treatment Strategies		$14.95	

Subtotal	
Tax Add (6.225% in MO and 5.00% in WY)	
Shipping Fee Add ($3.75 for the first book and $1.00 for each additional book)	
Total Amount	

3   **Payment Method:** Telephone Orders/Toll Free: 1(800)408-8830 • Fax Orders to: 1(816)587-7198
Send Postal Orders to: Compact Clinicals • 7205 NW Waukomis Dr., Suite A • Kansas City, MO 64151

☐ Check Enclosed
☐ Please charge to my:
   ○ Visa   Name on Card
   ○ MasterCard   Cardholder Signature
                    Account #/Exp. Date   _ _ _ _ - _ _ _ _ - _ _ _ _ - _ _ _ _ (_ _/_ _)

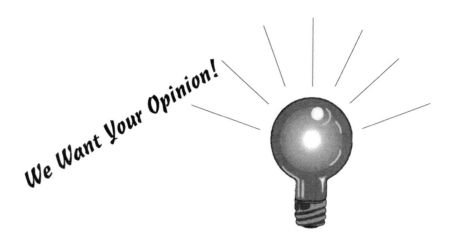

We Want Your Opinion!

Comments about the book: _____

Name of Book

_____

_____

_____

_____

Other titles you want Compact Clinicals to offer:

_____

_____

_____

Please provide your name and address in the space below to be placed on our mailing list.

_____

_____

_____

_____

Compact Clinicals

Ordering in three easy steps:
Order 24 hours a day: 1(800)408-8830

1   **Please fill out completely:**

Billing/Shipping Information

Individual/Company   Department/Mail Stop
_____

Street Address/P.O. Box
_____

City, State, Zip
_____

Telephone
_____

2   **Here's what I'd like to order:**

Book Name	Book Qty.	Unit Price	Total
Attention Deficit Hyperactivity Disorder (in Adults and Children) The Latest Assessment and Treatment Strategies		$14.95	
Borderline Personality Disorder The Latest Assessment and Treatment Strategies		$14.95	
Conduct Disorders The Latest Assessment and Treatment Strategies		$14.95	
Major Depressive Disorder The Latest Assessment and Treatment Strategies		$14.95	
Obsessive Compulsive Disorder The Latest Assessment and Treatment Strategies		$14.95	
		Subtotal	
	Tax Add (6.225% in MO and 5.00% in WY)		
		Shipping Fee	
	Add ($3.75 for the first book and $1.00 for each additional book)		
		Total Amount	

3   **Payment Method:** Telephone Orders/Toll Free: 1(800)408-8830 • Fax Orders to: 1(816)587-7198
Send Postal Orders to: Compact Clinicals • 7205 NW Waukomis Dr., Suite A • Kansas City, MO 64151

☐ Check Enclosed
☐ Please charge to my:
  ○ Visa   Name on Card   _____
  ○ MasterCard   Cardholder Signature _____
                  Account #/Exp. Date   _ _ _ _ - _ _ _ _ - _ _ _ _ - _ _ _ _ (_ _/_ _)

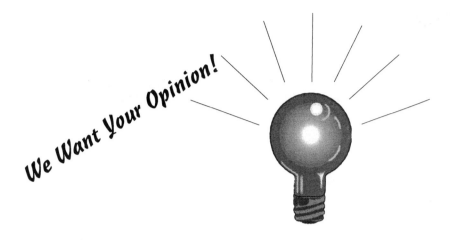

We Want Your Opinion!

Comments about the book: _____

Name of Book

_____

_____

_____

_____

Other titles you want Compact Clinicals to offer:

_____

_____

_____

_____

Please provide your name and address in the space below to be placed on our mailing list.

_____

_____

_____

_____

Compact Clinicals

Ordering in three easy steps:

Order 24 hours a day: 1(800)408-8830

1   **Please fill out completely:**

Billing/Shipping Information

Individual/Company   Department/Mail Stop

Street Address/P.O. Box

City, State, Zip

Telephone

2   **Here's what I'd like to order:**

Book Name	Book Qty.	Unit Price	Total
Attention Deficit Hyperactivity Disorder (in Adults and Children) The Latest Assessment and Treatment Strategies		$14.95	
Borderline Personality Disorder The Latest Assessment and Treatment Strategies		$14.95	
Conduct Disorders The Latest Assessment and Treatment Strategies		$14.95	
Major Depressive Disorder The Latest Assessment and Treatment Strategies		$14.95	
Obsessive Compulsive Disorder The Latest Assessment and Treatment Strategies		$14.95	

Subtotal	
Tax Add (6.225% in MO and 5.00% in WY)	
Shipping Fee Add ($3.75 for the first book and $1.00 for each additional book)	
Total Amount	

3   **Payment Method:** Telephone Orders/Toll Free: 1(800)408-8830 • Fax Orders to: 1(816)587-7198

Send Postal Orders to: Compact Clinicals • 7205 NW Waukomis Dr., Suite A • Kansas City, MO 64151

☐ Check Enclosed
☐ Please charge to my:
    ◯ Visa   Name on Card   _____
    ◯ MasterCard   Cardholder Signature
                 Account #/Exp. Date   _ _ _ _ - _ _ _ _ - _ _ _ _ - _ _ _ _ (_ _/_ _)